"Dr. Nancy Meyer's book, *Defyi brace Your True Value*, is incre advice for those who have exper. their faith and worth. She draws on biblical truths, well-known quotes, and personal experiences that allow her readers to experience sustainable breakthroughs and fulfillment and success in life."

—**MARK LONG**, Fellowship of Christian Athletes,
Leader FCA Endurance

"In *Defying Fear: Finding the Courage to Embrace Your True Value*, Dr. Nancy Meyer captures your interest immediately. Though the story is fiction by literal standards, it grips you even more when you know it is all based on fact. She has taken parts of many women's true stories to create a compilation character she calls Lila.

This story is startling, sometimes scary, with moments of surprising humor. But what I found most gratifying was how inspired this book left me. Yes, Lila endures unfair abuse, but she proves to us that when we defy fear, we can learn to courageously embrace our true value. I am stronger in mind, body, and spirit because I read this book. As Dr. Meyer reminds us, we all have a little Lila inside of us, including the best parts."

—**ANITA AGERS-BROOKS**, international speaker,
common trauma expert, and best-selling author of
Getting Through What You Can't Get Over and other titles

"Dr. Nancy Meyer has painted a portrait of a true heroine in *Defying Fear: Finding the Courage to Embrace Your True Value*. Her composite character Lila is an avatar who embodies the very soul of a survivor. This heartbreaking story of physical and mental abuse will strike a familiar note with women of the Me Too era. Lila will inspire those who endure the pain, suffering, and desolation of domestic abuse and who discover their inner strength, overcome fear, and bravely forge a new path toward self-fulfillment. Lila encourages readers not just to survive but to thrive and strive for their personal best."

—**M. C. CANNON**, nonprofit developer

"It is such an honor to endorse this amazing book. Dr. Nancy Meyer has a very experienced, multifaceted story, and in the spirit of helping others, shares her wisdom. I wish I had a resource of this magnitude while trying to navigate life when mine fell apart. I felt as though my family and I were on an island. Knowing you're not alone because someone overcame and was victorious gives one hope.

Dr. Nancy has mastered business, parenting, exercise, nutrition, and much more through her strength, perseverance, and spirituality. This book is a much needed wealth of knowledge. Many counselors know what they've learned from education. Nancy's firsthand experience will have an impact on countless lives and create a positive ripple effect. All of us encounter obstacles in life. Nancy provides a blueprint of how to survive and thrive. It had to be difficult to revisit the darkest of times in her life. I'm thankful for Dr. Nancy Meyer's strength and keeping the faith!"

—**GINGER MUMPOWER**, Ginger's Jewelry

"I could not put this book down! Dr. Meyer does an amazing job of bringing to life the character of Lila. I felt an immediate connection to her from experiences in my own life. Although my memories were painful to relive as strong emotions were brought back as I followed Lila's struggles, the journey helped me reflect on myself and my own growth. Lila navigates through horrible forms of emotional abuse as well as the harsh retaliatory malice of her husband. Amazingly, she does all of this with grace and respect out of love for her children, and finally for herself! She leans on her faith and her weaknesses grow into unstoppable strengths—support of a higher power, God. This book reminds us that God is good; we all are deserving of love, we have value, and as his children we are strengthened by him. I'm not necessarily a religious person, but this message really struck home. Thank you, Nancy, for sharing your words with us."

—**KATHRYN DAVIS**, Nursing Practice & Clinical Integrations Manager, MSN, RN; Roanoke Triathlon Club, President

"This is a gut-wrenching story of heartache, betrayal, and loss. It is also a hope-filled story of acceptance, resilience, and renewal. Dr. Nancy Meyer takes readers on a fictional journey that is grounded in true experiences and real life. She also weaves in practical advice that is helpful, inspirational, and biblical. Throughout this book, your faith will grow as you discover God's love and mercy in life's difficulties and trials."

—SETH BRYANT, Lead Pastor, New Hope Christian Church

"*Defying Fear: Finding the Courage to Embrace Your True Value* is a moving and inspirational story of a woman who battles gaslighting/emotional trauma for years before discovering the strength to persevere and overcome her fears. Her ever-deepening faith and reliance on God slowly leads her to restoration and newfound strength. Although this book deals with difficult issues, the reader is led through godly bits of wisdom at the end of each chapter that inspire hope for a better future. This is a wonderful book for any woman who has experienced abusive relationships or anyone mentoring a friend through these situations."

—PATRICIA V. CUNNINGHAM, PhD, immunology; former research scientist; President, LEEPS Foundation

"Occasionally one will be reading a book, and the words of the author will leap off the page and the reader will find a part of themselves expressed in the author's written words, opening an awareness of something in their own life they never realized before. Dr. Nancy Meyer, in *Defying Fear: Finding the Courage to Embrace Your True Value*, does just this through her character Lila. Abuse is such a difficult topic and equally difficult to heal from. God can use our stories to do what only He can do, and Lila, though initially unaware of her identity as a victim of abuse, in part by sharing her story, was able to overcome her fear and leave us an example of how to heal and become who God intends us to be. I believe this book will speak to many readers as it has spoken to me."

—MELINDA JACKSON, MD, PhD, FAAFP

"I have had the pleasure of knowing Nancy Meyer for several years. She's smart, kind, caring, and an amazing author. But most of all she is a child of God and a true believer even in the face of life completely unraveling.

Nancy's stories and illustrations cut straight to your heart as she narrates the tales of women who have experienced deep fear and how they overcame some of the worst despair anyone could experience. Those who read this book will walk away with the feeling of being able to overcome anything, to pull yourself through any crisis, and to overcome any fear that may be holding you back.

As Nancy notes at the end of the book, we *CAN do all things through Christ*. This book is written by one of the strongest women I know, and is a must-read for anyone who needs the courage to face any foreboding moments life may bring."

—DR. MICHAEL PERUSICH, motivational speaker

"In Dr. Nancy Meyer's new book, *Defying Fear: Finding the Courage to Embrace Your True Value*, the reader is quickly pulled into an intimate emotional relationship with the main character, Lila, who, through a series of sequential scenarios, pulls you along with her from victim to conqueror.

The format of the book is very helpful as each chapter describes a difficult experience followed by relevant Scripture containing very practical application of those verses. Each reader will be both challenged and encouraged in their personal journey of faith. This is a book that I will be recommending to help many clients work through their own traumas and discover their true worth. It's a wonderful, wonderful testimony."

—MRS. DARNELL T. BARNES, licensed clinical social worker and
certified substance abuse counselor

"In *Defying Fear: Finding the Courage to Embrace Your True Value*, Dr. Nancy Meyer presents a compelling account of fear, heartache, anger, humiliation, betrayal, and other numerous emotional phases. Presented as a fictional story, it connects with the reality of life reaching into the world of many women. The characters depict real-life situations that the main character, Lila, is faced with regarding the many choices she had to make.

During this fearful adventure she is guided through trusted advice and faith to how one is able to overcome fear and find courage. Her courage in suffering when innocent and to protect her children, business, and reputation will challenge those who read this book to rise above the injustice and fear to find the courage to embrace your true value."

—ELWOOD MCALLISTER, retired minister

*D*edicated to all the people still hanging on and refusing to give up in spite of life's heartaches.

You are inspirational!

Remember to
Defy Fear,
Find Courage,
Embrace Your Value!

Be Courageous,
Dr. Nancy Meyer

Dr. Nancy Meyer

DEFYING
fear

Finding the Courage
to Embrace Your True Value

BROOKSTONE
PUBLISHING GROUP

Defying Fear

Brookstone Publishing Group
An imprint of Iron Stream Media
100 Missionary Ridge
Birmingham, AL 35242
IronStreamMedia.com

Library of Congress Control Number: 2023900923

Cover design and interior typeset by twolineStudio.com

ISBN: 978-1-949856-96-5 (paperback)
ISBN: 978-1-949856-97-2 (eBook)

1 2 3 4 5—27 26 25 24 23

INTRODUCTION

*S*ix months into my divorce, I woke up to a bright blue, sun-filled sky—the scent of coming rain filled the air. The weather matched my energy, as my soul rejoiced with fresh hope.

That night, just after putting my eleven-year-old son to bed at 9:00 p.m., a knock on my door stripped me of my peace.

"You've been served," the officer said.

I looked at him and said, "What is this?"

He explained it was a protective order filed against me for stalking. He sauntered down the sidewalk while I tried to absorb the confusion and fear that consumed me. I looked toward the moon and stars and cried out, "Is this ever going to end?"

The stalking charges and protective order against me meant my kids and I were still not safe. Coming within three hundred feet of my daughter could result in my arrest for a Class 1 misdemeanor, and I could spend a year in jail if I violated the order. Prior to this, I'd never even gotten a speeding ticket.

The fight for custody of my kids became one of my lowest points—and the situation would get worse.

Months later, everything changed when my attorney called. "Congratulations, you've got your kids back."

When I tried to ask him a few questions and if I should go get my kids, he said, "Be the !@#$% parent and get your !@#$% kids."

I decided to pick up my daughter after an athletic event at her high school. I had won a battle, but the war was far from over.

Later that day, my mom, my identical twin sister, and I sat on a bleacher at the high school gym cheering my daughter's volleyball team. Movement in my peripheral vision made me turn my head. The particular group of people walking in signaled trouble. Trying to avoid it, I slipped out a side door into a hallway, in hopes they hadn't seen me. Obviously, it didn't work. When I heard the sirens in the distance and the police showed up a few minutes later, I knew someone had reported me.

I walked out to take responsibility and meet the situation head-on. My mom and sister stood next to me. But a problem immediately presented itself.

From the moment the police arrived, you could tell the bad cop from the good one. The short, stocky male spoke roughly and rudely. He looked at my sister. "Are you Nancy Meyer?"

Nearly hysterical, she said, "No."

He looked at me. "So, you're Ms. Meyer?"

"Yes," I said.

"You're being arrested for stalking and violation of a protective order," he said in an overly authoritative voice. He snapped the cuffs around my wrists.

The female officer stepped into the chaos, acting firmly, but with respect and kindness. She guided me toward the squad car and dipped my head down and gently forced me inside.

The parking lot was full of people there to watch the game. Onlookers gathered quickly. Parents of kids I'd coached. Friends. Humiliation and panic fought for control of my emotions. Then I remembered my back pocket.

After several seconds of wriggling and squirming, I managed to get my cell phone in my hand. I shifted sideways and dialed a friend who knew my attorney and asked her to reach out to him. Desperate for help, I called a couple other friends.

The police officer checked on me in the back of her car. She saw me talking on my cell while I held it awkwardly in my fingertips. "I've never seen anyone make phone calls with their hands cuffed behind their back before." I was not thrilled to be first in this category.

The drive to the jail made me feel closed in and claustrophobic. There's nothing worse than knowing you are completely helpless, unable to free yourself, especially when you don't know where your kids are. By the time we arrived at the police station, the handcuffs were digging into my skin. Despite my discomfort, booking officers took my mug shot and fingerprinted me. I had a new understanding of why so many people scowl in their mug shots.

I was taken to an adjoining room and placed on a bench to sit and wait. But I had no idea what I was waiting for. After a while, I was taken into a hearing area, where a magistrate oversaw proceedings. He looked at me. "You sure have a bucketload of people here." He nodded toward the gaggle of family and friends there showing support. It must have made an impact.

The magistrate did something unheard of—he released me that night.

A few hours later, I went home and dropped on my couch feeling spent. But I wasn't alone.

A sizeable number of people showed up to sit with me. They surrounded me, literally and figuratively. Everyone wanted to know how they could help, and I was grateful for their concern. One friend tried to reduce my heartache with a little humor. "Did you make me a customized license plate?"

I laughed and immediately broke down. I wondered, *How can this be happening to me? All I want is to be with my kids.*

Later that evening, my attorney called, but I immediately sensed his disapproval. His cool demeanor made me feel like I had as a little girl when I let my mom down. The lawyer confirmed his feelings when he said, "This is your fault. You shouldn't have gone to that school."

I was so confused by his words until I found out the reason behind the confusion. When my attorney had told me I had won custody of my kids, he neglected to reveal that it was only a verbal agreement and had not yet been officially filed with the courts. This omission would lead to a whole other level of nightmare.

Again, I wondered if I was unworthy of happiness or freedom from fear. I felt deserving of the shame and guilt that consumed me. Familiar feelings of abandonment and rejection overtook me. I didn't yet realize my PTSD, anxiety, and depression had been triggered. I was so sad. I had no energy. My normally positive outlook had been stolen from me. I didn't want to eat. I didn't want to drink. I couldn't sleep. I wanted to die. The only reason I didn't act on my desire to give up was my maternal instinct to protect and fight for my children.

Since being arrested, I've spoken to many women who have their own horror stories about betrayal, abuse, rejection, abandonment, anxiety, depression, and PTSD. Many, like me, have felt unworthy and unlovable. But this is not God's plan for them, me, or you.

In this book, I am pulling from multiple women's real stories to write a compiled fictional account built on a foundation of solid truth. To protect the innocent and at-risk, I am using a disguised character whom I call Lila. The events and outcomes happened. The lessons are valid, even when they came from a mixture of many women's experiences. Although Lila is not a real person, she is a true persona based on real people. I think most if not all women have a little Lila in them.

If you can relate to any of the experiences or feelings you will read about, I want you to hold on to hope. Grip your faith. With a tight fist. I assure you, if I can survive the events of my life and come out on top, you can do the same.

And you are meant to. You are worthy of good things. You are worthy of feeling valued. Regardless of your past and what you've thought or been told, it's time for you to let the truth seep in. You are deserving of happiness, joy, and love.

You are meant to defy fear.

I pray it doesn't take as much time or therapy for you as it did for me to realize my own value. Thankfully, God's grace and patience are unending. But none of that would soak in until I went through much more pain—similar to Lila's.

CHAPTER ONE

ALL IN HER
Head

*F.E.A.R. has two meanings: Fear everything
and run or face everything and rise.*

—ZIG ZIGLAR

*A*fter feeling beaten down for months and years, Lila's hope flickered. Her husband, L. T., sounded unusually chipper one morning during breakfast. "Want to go to the gym with me this morning?"

Maybe the new year means a fresh start. Happy New Year to us, Lila thought. She smiled. "I'd love to. Let me change into my workout clothes."

L. T. didn't respond and stared at her with an unidentifiable expression.

A couple of minutes later, Lila exited their bedroom feeling more excited than she had in ages. She checked the house and realized her husband was gone. "L. T.?" she called out.

No answer.

Lila walked out to the garage and sighed. His car was gone.

A familiar hurt crept into Lila's soul. She got into her own vehicle and drove to the gym—alone, feeling confused and afraid. She should have known.

When Lila arrived, she found her husband riding a stationary bike. Sounding more desperate than angry, she said, "You couldn't wait five minutes for me?"

L. T. ignored her, as if Lila wasn't even standing there. His previous cheeriness did not match his current disregard for her or her feelings. This type of chronic disrespect summed up their relationship. Lila had a partner in name but not in practice. However, as much as she'd been through up to that moment, Lila still hadn't discovered the full extent of her husband's degrading acts toward her. His upcoming big announcement would reveal even more.

Three days later, on January 2, Lila worked from her home office. Before 7:00 a.m. she filed the year-end payroll tax reports, earlier than usual. She also submitted the employee W-2 forms.

Their young poodle, Sammy, lay by her feet, happy to be out of the laundry room. When her husband was home, the pup wasn't allowed in any other room of the house.

As Lila finished up, L. T. walked in. He saw Sammy, but instead of grousing, he ignored the dog. "I'm going to take your car in to get the heater fixed. I need to do it before you make the nine-hour drive to your mom's house when your grandpa dies."

The matter-of-factness of L. T.'s tone stung, even as she marveled that he cared about her comfort at all. He'd never offered to fix anything on her car before. Lila's ninety-one-year-old grandpa was fighting an infection and had C. diff. Like others who battle the affliction, her grandfather had severe diarrhea. He was severely dehydrated and probably had only a few days left to live.

"Heath asked me to take him shopping at the mall today," Lila said. "I'd like to get him new shoes before I have to leave, and his school break ends next week."

"I know; he told me. You can take my car," L. T. said.

Lila pursed her lips. "OK." She again wondered about her husband's yo-yoing behavior.

Later, Lila learned the real reason L. T. wanted her SUV. As soon as Lila and Heath left for the mall, her husband came back to the house and removed their safe from the bedroom closet. The safe weighed around 150 pounds and wouldn't fit into his small sports car.

When he arrived home after 5:00 p.m. that evening, L. T. told Lila the dealership worked on her car all day. She found out later they really started at 12:30 and finished by 2:00 p.m. He had spent the missing afternoon hours meeting one of his mistresses at a local Barnes & Noble. His narcissism did not end there. Lila simply wasn't aware of any of this yet.

After Lila's husband arrived from "getting the car fixed" he told her his back was killing him from moving the Christmas tree into the attic at their shared medical office. They were both sports medicine practitioners with an emphasis on college athletes. Lila felt bad for L. T., so she adjusted him at home, not knowing he injured his back removing their safe. She also didn't realize he had gathered all the keys for his car and the extra keys to hers.

On Sunday, Lila and L. T. went to church with their kids, twelve-year-old Heath and six-year-old Grace, as they typically did. In their almost twenty years together, physical touch with L. T. occurred only in church when they held hands and privately when he wanted sex. But on that day, he would not touch her in public, even at church. He rebuffed every one of her attempts.

What did I do? Why is he so mad at me? Lila placed her arm next to L. T.'s leg, nudged him gently, and tried yet again to get her husband to hold her hand. He ignored her and focused on the preacher as if she wasn't in the sanctuary. After the service, they drove home in silence.

Later that afternoon, Lila tried to focus on some paperwork in their office. She hoped the familiar would drown out the voice of concern over her husband's worsening see-saw attitude. *What am I doing wrong? How can I fix things between us? Why won't he love me?*

L. T. breezed in. "Hey babe, do you think you could adjust me again? My lower back really hurts."

Lila's first instinct was to say no and to express her own hurt over how he'd treated her in church that morning. How could he act like nothing happened? Fearing a blow up, she sighed, got out of her chair, and walked toward the adjusting table.

After she finished, L. T. hopped up. He shocked Lila by asking for something he had never requested in their nearly twenty years as a couple.

"Could we go over our home budget?"

Caught off guard, Lila stammered, not because she had anything to hide but because she had tried to get L. T. to take an active role in their finances for years. She wanted him to show an interest in money beyond what it could get him.

An hour later, after reviewing the numbers, Lila thought L. T. finally understood what she had been trying to tell him for weeks. They'd experienced an income dip in their practice and money was very tight. Years of trying to keep up with L. T.'s excessive spending coupled with what seemed to be his weakening work ethics had caught up with them.

For many months, L. T. had made himself available to see patients on only Mondays, Wednesdays, and Fridays, yet he frequently took four-hour lunch breaks so he could play golf. Or at least that's what he said he was doing. And he usually left early every Friday.

Lila saw patients on Tuesdays and Thursdays, plus covered for L. T. on the other days, while managing the entire office and their personal household. She lived with mental, emotional, and physical fatigue trying to juggle everything.

Over dinner that evening, L. T. surprised his wife yet again. "Know what, kids?"

"What?" their son and daughter chimed together.

"The best part of my day was the good meal Mommy made."

The kids cheered and Sammy barked.

Lila's eyebrows instinctively furrowed. She couldn't keep up with the whiplash of L. T.'s changing moods. The night before, he hadn't eaten a bite after she fixed his favorite meal. He scraped every last bite of beef Stroganoff into the trash. Lila still didn't know what set him off. She made sure every room was clean before he got home and thought she had everything the way he liked it.

But now, as if reading her mind, L. T. locked eyes with her and grinned like a Cheshire cat.

Lila's mind swirled. *One minute he's yelling at me, then the next he says something nice. Is he intentionally messing with my mind? He loves me, he loves me not. What am I supposed to believe? Is L. T. right, is this all in my head?*

Deep down, Lila knew something was wrong. But without proof to validate her feelings, she felt helpless. Pushing back was pointless. She didn't realize she'd become so stuck in her conditioned role of peacemaker that she'd lost her ability to separate truth from lies or to create and hold appropriate boundaries when they were needed. She had numbed her own voice.

The next day, L. T. went to their practice, about fifteen minutes from their home. Lila didn't yet know what he was capable of. She would soon find herself feeling like she did a few years earlier when she discovered his secret depravity and betrayal.

BREAKING FEAR'S HOLD

Too many people are bound by the kinds of fear Lila felt imprisoned by and do not realize they are in the stronghold of an abusive relationship. They don't dare question or stand up, even when obvious issues with their spouses, bosses, clients, or even their children are shouting to be heard.

It's easy to discount a warning voice in an effort to believe what you want to be true. But don't ditch what you think or feel or discount what your heart knows. Address your concerns. Ask your questions. Investigate. Believe in your ability to recognize and assess when situations don't line up with what you're being told.

There is no shame in loving someone. But remember, real love casts out all fear (1 John 4:18). You shouldn't have to constantly tiptoe around people you are in a relationship with. If something feels off or you fear telling people what you're going through, this is a red flag you need to acknowledge.

You are not in a good situation. Ask God to reveal the truth. Nothing is hidden with Him.

*Call to me and I will answer you
and tell you great and unsearchable things
you do not know.*

—JEREMIAH 33:3

CHAPTER TWO

ILLUSION AND
Images

*Courage doesn't always roar. Sometimes
courage is a quiet voice at the end of the day
saying, "I will try again tomorrow."*

—MARY ANNE RADMACHER

*L*ila grew up hearing the message, both verbally and subliminally, that sex was bad. This conditioning made her husband's violation even more painful. Eventually, even she would come to wonder how she stayed with him after the way he dishonored her and desecrated their marriage.

After picking six-year-old Grace up from school, Lila pulled into her parking space at Frost & Frost Sports Medicine. This was her first stop in a series of errands she needed to run with her daughter in tow.

Lila breezed up to the receptionist area. "How's the day going?" she asked her front desk staff.

A natural extrovert, Julianna, answered for the group of three workers. "Great! Dr. Frost is in treatment room five adjusting a patient right now. He should be done in ten minutes or so." She pointed a burgundy acrylic nail toward the door across the hall.

"Terrific," Lila said. "I don't really need to see him. But I do need to grab some paperwork from his office. Keep up the good work. I appreciate you guys." Grabbing Grace by the hand, Lila headed to her husband's office at the back of the building.

She pushed the door open and stopped. The computer monitor faced the entryway, and what she saw on it made her knees buckle beneath her.

Even though discomfort made her quickly turn away, she couldn't miss the naked woman sprawled across L. T.'s computer screen. Curiosity made her look again. This time, she focused her eyes on the face of the naked woman. She looked familiar. She covered her mouth with her hand.

Why did he have a picture of me? On his computer? At work?

Lila turned away. Cold sweat beaded on her upper lip. Dizziness came in waves as questions bounced around her brain.

Why would my husband do something so perverted?

Am I imagining this?

Am I having a nightmare?

Lila snapped back to reality at Grace's question.

"Mommy, is that you?"

Lila wanted to cry, but didn't dare upset her daughter, so she lied. "No, honey, that isn't me." Lila gently turned Grace by the shoulders and ushered her to the chair beside the desk, away from the computer screen. Lila absently handed Grace her tablet to play with, before going back to investigate more closely.

Lila looked closer at the text on the screen. It described her body in lewd detail, followed with a message that read, "If you like what you see, contact me. Let's meet." Still struggling to believe what she was seeing, Lila snapped a picture of the computer screen.

Why is L. T. posting my picture on the internet? How could my husband do this to me?

Grace giggled at something on the video she was watching. Suddenly, protecting her daughter overshadowed anything else on Lila's mind. She grabbed her little girl by the wrist and almost ran into L. T. in the hallway as he exited treatment room five. Their eyes met. She glared at him.

He glanced toward his open office door then stared at her as if daring her to challenge him.

Lila opened her mouth to speak but decided against saying anything with Grace there. Breathe. Just breathe. She repeated the mantra to herself again. Breathe!

The silence between husband and wife grew clumsier. Lila felt the eyes of staff members on them, though her embarrassment would not allow her to look around. She mumbled, "I've got to get home. I need to start supper."

L. T. nodded without altering the expression on his face.

"Say goodbye to Daddy, Grace," Lila said.

"Bye, Daddy."

L. T. swooped their daughter into his arms. "Who's Daddy's best girl?" He tickled Grace's ribs.

Feeling uncomfortable, Lila interrupted. "We need to go, Grace. Let your father get back to work." She knew she sounded harsh.

Grace whined. "Why can't we stay a little longer?"

L. T. nuzzled Grace's neck and whispered loud enough to make sure Lila heard him too. "Go ahead, pumpkin. You know Mommy always kills our fun."

Lila shook her head. Per usual, he painted Lila as the bad guy.

When L. T. arrived home that evening, he acted as if the day's earlier event hadn't taken place. Lila wanted to raise the issue, but she didn't want to create conflict in front of the kids either. She also wanted to investigate more and talk to a couple of friends first. Lila swallowed hard and joined in the pretense that all was well in their home. She would restrain herself until the weekend.

The next day, L. T. had the day off and would be shuttling the kids around, so Lila took advantage of his absence and went to the office early, before staff and patients could keep her from her mission. It didn't take long for her to figure out L. T.'s passwords and checked his internet history. The images she found sickened her but not as much as her husband's graphic measurements and descriptions of her private body parts. Why would anyone want to know her nipple size?

The more she found, the more Lila felt as if she were being repeatedly raped by her husband and complete strangers. But she pushed through. She had to know the full extent of what L. T. had done.

In one chat, pretending to be Lila, L. T. posted: "Is it bad that I'm not willing to share my husband but my husband is willing to share me?"

Lila thought about the many times L. T. had tried to get her to agree to having another woman in their bed, but Lila had staunchly refused. She waffled between anger and guilt. *Did I drive my husband to this by refusing to give him what he wanted?*

After nearly an hour of discovering betrayal after betrayal, Lila dropped her elbows on the desktop and laid her forehead in her hands. Fighting against tears and a swelling anxiety attack, myriad thoughts pummeled her mind: *Who all has seen these? How can I go out in public?*

When done, Lila printed several vile images from the computer.

Later that afternoon, she met her friend Cindy for tea and showed the photos to her.

Cindy's response was swift and pointed. "This is unacceptable. No man should do this to his wife."

"That's what I thought at first," Lila said. "But then I questioned myself."

"Look, I don't want to hurt your feelings, but you defend and justify L. T.'s inappropriateness constantly. It's time you quit."

Lila nodded. It was time to face off with her husband.

On Saturday, Lila arranged for the kids to spend the night with friends. She was determined to make L. T. discuss the situation with her, and she vowed not to be manipulated.

"We need to talk," she said and pointed toward the dining room table.

"I'm getting ready to go work out," L. T. shot back but sat anyway.

"What made you think you could share those pictures of me with complete strangers? And why did you invite people to meet while you pretended to be me? I didn't even want you to take those pictures. You talked me into it. And they were supposed to be private—just between us!"

L. T. shrugged. "Seemed like you were into it at the time."

Lila noticed how he avoided addressing the privacy issue. She absolutely did not want him to take those photos of her. How *did* he talk her into it? Lila sat back and reflected on that night.

She'd just finished putting the kids to bed. It surprised her when L. T. offered to get her a glass of water. Lila should have questioned his thoughtfulness, but instead, she hoped it was a sign of change. Lila sat on the couch, accepted the water, and smiled after taking a long drink. "Thank you."

She placed the glass on the end table and noticed a light pink tinge to the liquid. She blinked intentionally. *My eyes must be playing with the room lighting*, she thought. She took another drink. Tasted OK.

The warm, relaxing sensation hit her first. The living room swayed ever so slightly. Or was it Lila's body that undulated?

L. T. spoke but he sounded like a robot under water talking in slow motion. "Hooow aarrre yooou feeeeliiing, baaabe?"

Lila's voice sounded equally muddled to her ringing ears. "I. Feel. Funny."

"Just roll with it," L. T. said. "Relax and enjoy. Let's take some pictures."

"Pictures?"

"Yeah. I'll show you what I want."

"I don't like pictures of myself."

"Don't you want to please me?" L. T. said. "Don't you want to make me happy? Don't you love me?"

Those were the magic questions that pushed Lila's buttons. He knew them all. The warmth in her veins seemed to heighten. "OK. I'll do it for you."

They moved to the bedroom, and L. T. jumped at the chance to play photographer. "Lift your arms. Pull your hair up. Stick your chest out."

Lila's normal inhibitions seemed to flutter away the second they crossed her mind.

"Stretch out on the bed. Touch yourself," L. T. smiled. "Yeah, that's right, baby."

In her drowsy state, Lila had a distant awareness of what was taking place. Time blurred. She didn't even know how many pictures L. T. took.

Now sitting at the table across from her husband, an epiphany struck. She realized L. T. had done something to her, and he displayed no remorse or embarrassment for his actions. "You drugged me."

"I didn't drug you."

"That's how you got me to go along with those pictures. You slipped something in my water. You did drug me!"

"That? I just gave you a little something to loosen you up. I simply helped you relax so you could get into the mood. And it was hot! You were the best that night." L. T.'s grin did nothing to ease Lila's anxious mind.

"How could you do that to me?" she cried. "I'm your wife."

"What? Show you a good time? You've got issues if you can't appreciate a husband like me." L. T. shrugged. "I'm leaving. I don't know what time I'll be back. Don't wait up."

Guilt rose in Lila's gut, triggered by L. T.'s accusation. She longed to be loved by her husband and had tried everything she knew to make him want her for who she was, not as a sex toy. The only thing she had ever said no to was allowing someone else in their bedroom. But it seemed Lila could never do enough to quench her husband's salacious desires.

Lila had put up with so much through the years, believing L. T.'s reasoning and explanations when she felt scared or uncomfortable. But Lila wondered what part of her husband's brain told him it was OK to expose her intimately without her permission. And how did her supposedly computer-illiterate husband learn how to upload those images, add text, and share them in chat rooms?

When L. T. came to bed later that night, he said nothing, and began snoring minutes later. Lila, however, tossed and turned. Her sleeplessness made even worse because of her husband's callousness. He could snooze through anything, even if hell froze over.

The next morning, L. T. cheerily announced he was going to the golf course before seeing his first patient at 2:00 p.m. He walked out unfazed by the previous night's events.

L. T.'s behavior would normally frustrate Lila, but today she was glad he would arrive to work later than normal. She had a lot to think about.

What if someone believed she posted those perverted pictures when L. T. pretended to be her? Could that cause Child Protective Services to show up?

Lila knew she had to get a handle on her emotions. She searched for counselors in the area and took the first available appointment. Later, she told L. T. but didn't expect him to agree to go. He shocked her when he said he would.

After they entered the therapist's office, Mr. Tim Musse swept his arm toward the chairs across from his desk, inviting them to sit. The scent of sandalwood tickled Lila's nose.

At the counselor's prompting, years of anguish poured from Lila. "Even though I'm married, I feel so lonely. I feel violated.

I trusted L. T. with my mind, soul, and body, and I feel like I'm meaningless to him. I'm not enough. He's on porn sites. He used a date rape drug on me and shared intimate pictures of me with strangers.

"Every time I think about people looking at those images, I feel like I'm being raped. Tell me, how can I care so much for someone who hurts me so deeply? I want to feel loved, to feel missed if I disappeared. I want to feel cherished. But I don't get any of that from my husband."

Without acknowledging any of Lila's concerns directly, the therapist said, "L. T., what is your perspective on what your wife just said?"

"I don't deny what she's telling you, but I was thinking of her. I just wanted to please my wife sexually and help her feel better about herself. It seems like no matter what I do she finds fault with me. She doesn't desire me like a wife should. Sometimes, I can't help wondering if she isn't really gay and won't admit it to herself or to me."

Lila's jaw dropped. L. T. had tried the "gay" tactic with her before, when he wanted her to participate in a threesome. His pressure to make her admit this untruth privately was one thing, but surely the therapist would kibosh it once and for all.

Mr. Musse tapped the side of his lips with his index finger. "Lila, did you ever consider that maybe your husband was doing all of this for you? That he was placing you on a pedestal and trying to do what he thought you wanted? He probably should have communicated better, but it sounds like his intentions were in the right place. A man needs to know his wife desires him."

Lila couldn't believe her ears. She heard the words but felt like she was watching from another room. Numbness flooded her every cell. Instead of validating what she'd been through, the counselor blamed her too.

The rest of the session, Lila contemplated in silence while the therapist and L. T. conversed. She doubted either of them noticed. *I can't believe this counselor is agreeing with everything L. T. says. Even I know this isn't right.*

For days afterward, Lila felt self-conscious thinking others were looking at her wherever she went—at the grocery store, gas station, Walmart. She wanted to hide, imagining everyone she encountered knew her secret shame.

Lila felt a need to protect her husband. She didn't want people to think L. T. was awful or to look down on him. Lila cried until her eyes were swollen.

Four days after the disastrous counselor's visit, she woke up in the early morning hours, went into her closet, kneeled, and prayed. She sensed God telling her not to be ashamed and assuring her that if others found out she should simply tell the truth about what happened.

A few hours later, she called her friend Angela. They agreed to meet at the Smoothie Queen down the street from Lila's house.

Angela was already seated when Lila walked in. "Hey girl, I'm so glad you called."

Lila clutched her friend in a hug while tears poured off her chin.

"You all right?" Angela said, brushing Lila's cheeks.

"Not really." Without pause, Lila dumped the story of her recent discoveries in Angela's lap. "I've tried to be a good wife. I even have sex with him four times a day."

"Four times a day?" Angela held up four fingers for emphasis.

"Yes. Is that even normal?"

"For a rabbit."

"He'd take more, if I could handle it," Lila said. "And he almost always says 'Thank you' when we're done. It makes me feel like an object, not his wife." Lila leaned forward to whisper. "How often do you and your husband have sex?"

Angela chuckled. "Girl, we have a healthy sex life, but we aren't doing it four times a day. Not even close."

"But the counselor told me L. T. was the normal one. He said everything my husband did was for me—even taking the pictures after drugging me."

"He said what to you? A licensed therapist?"

Lila nodded.

"That's out of line, if not downright unethical. He should have validated you instead of making you out to be the one at fault." A hint of crimson tinged Angela's neck and ears.

"He made me feel violated all over again," Lila said.

"I can only imagine," Angela said. "Look, I'm not a professional, but I learned something in one of my Bible studies that you might find helpful. When you feel overwhelmed, don't try to tackle everything at once. Give yourself some grace. One woman told us she struggled with really low self-esteem and said she learned to start her day with an affirmation.

"Every morning, look at yourself in the mirror and say, 'God loves, values, and cherishes me. I am going to love, value, and cherish me today.' Then repeat that truth a minimum of two more times during the day, especially before you go to bed. I make sure I at least look in the mirror and say it each morning."

Lila nodded. "I'm not sure how talking to myself in a mirror could help, but I guess I could try it."

"Don't just try. Commit to it," Angela said gently. "You deserve to see yourself the way God sees you."

A couple of weeks later, after committing to the exercise, Lila realized L. T.'s actions hadn't changed, but she felt a little stronger, bolder, and more capable. Life with her husband was still difficult and his attempts to manipulate had not lessened, but she felt better able to handle things.

Though life's painful bouts with L. T. were far from over, Angela's guidance proved a good start. Lila was just beginning to unearth the authentic love she'd hungered for, and even more was yet to come. But before the path to her healing came to light, she had to navigate greater darkness.

The key was holding on and not giving up—especially when it seemed everything was being stripped away.

OVERCOMING THE UNIMAGINABLE

None of us knows what the next minute might bring. Maybe you won't experience the kind of defilement Lila did, but gut kicks happen to us all. Most of us are either going through a crisis, coming out of one, or getting ready to enter one. We just don't know it yet. However, unforeseen events do not have to drive you to disillusionment, despair, or depression. God still turns our ash heaps into crowns of beauty (Isaiah 61:3), when we invite Him into our circumstances and allow Him to do His healing work.

Someone else's choices may impact you, but that does not mean you are at fault. If you do have some responsibility in the situation, admit it boldly, apologize authentically, and seize every opportunity to make amends. The fact is, we all mess up sometimes, but that does not mean we are a mess. It merely means we are human. Every human is worthy of feeling loved, valued, and cherished. We just need reminders at times, especially when life gets tough.

Only I can tell you the future
before it even happens.

—ISAIAH 46:10 NLT

CHAPTER THREE

THE *Jerk*

When everything seems to be going against you, remember that the airplane takes off against the wind, not with it.

—HENRY FORD

*R*emnants of Lila's mascara-stained teardrops littered the page of her journal. *I'm crushed. I feel so alone, God. I have no one to talk to besides you. Please help me.*

The morning began calmly enough. Lila had started her day in front of the mirror speaking her affirmations. "God loves, values, and cherishes me. I am going to love, value, and cherish me today."

After lunch, Lila drove toward the park, singing with the radio while the kids played happily in the back seat. Until they didn't.

Six-year-old Grace suddenly shouted, "Jerk!"

"Well, you're a !@#$%," Heath shot back.

Lila pulled onto the shoulder of the road and slammed on the brakes. She swung around in her seat and scowled. "We do not use those kinds of words in our family. Where did you hear that language?"

"You," Heath said.

"You did not hear that from me," Lila said. "I do not say or use those words."

Grace chimed in. "Daddy does. When he's driving and talking to you on the phone, Mommy, and he doesn't like what you say, he puts his hand on the phone and tells us, 'Mommy's a jerk. Mommy's a !@#$%.' I know it's a bad word."

"You're right, those are bad words," Lila said. "Daddy shouldn't be using them. No one should."

"I'm sorry, Mommy," Grace said.

"Yeah," Heath added.

Lila sighed. "Thank you, kids. Let's just try to have a better day with no bad words. All right?"

"OK," they said in unison.

When they pulled into a space at the park, Lila unbuckled Grace's booster seat and smiled when her children sprinted toward the playground. Heath made a beeline for the slide. Grace chose the sandbox. With both children in sight, yet out of earshot, Lila hit send on her phone.

L. T. answered in a gruff tone. "Hey. I'm getting ready to start my workout."

"I need to talk to you about something."

Heath yelled from the top of the slide, "I'm going to break my speed record, Mom. Watch."

Lila nodded and waved, right before Heath swished to the bottom. With no other kids at the park to impress, Heath relaxed and had fun. She missed the sweet side of her boy.

"Well?" L. T. said.

Lila lowered her voice and clenched her jaw. "The kids tell me that when you're on the phone with me and you don't like what I say, you whisper that Mommy's a jerk or a !@#$%."

"I say it under my breath. But fine, I'll try to do better. Now, I need to get to my workout. You know how I am when I can't exercise."

Lila ignored L. T.'s brush off. "Directing your name calling about me to our children is not saying it under your breath. And it's not OK, even if no one heard you. How about not calling me names at all? You're always demanding respect, but I deserve respect too. You shouldn't treat anyone that way, but especially me. I am your wife."

"Can't you just nag me later? After I'm done working out? This is exactly why I need exercise, to work off the kind of stress you're causing me now. I hate it when you nag."

"Unreal." Lila sighed. "By all means, go work out."

He ended the call before Lila could even pull the phone away from her ear. Her mind raced. Shouldn't he have said, "I'm sorry, it won't happen again"?

Grace called out. "Mommy, come play in the sand with me."

"OK, baby," Lila said. "But remember, we can't stay too long, and Mommy can't get dirty. I have to go into the office in a little bit."

An hour later, Lila stepped into her next disaster. As soon as she entered the office, their bookkeeper, Tanya, said, "Have you got a minute?"

Unfortunately, Lila had heard this question before and had a pretty good idea what was coming next. Sure enough, when the office door closed, Tanya said, "I need to submit my two-week notice."

"May I ask why?" Lila crossed her hands in her lap. "You've only been with us four months, but I hoped you were happy. I know I've been thrilled with your work."

Tanya squirmed in her chair. "Well, um, I need to leave for personal reasons. I'd rather not talk about it."

"Understood," Lila said. "I wish you well in your future endeavors. Thank you for being part of our team."

For a second, it looked like Tanya was about to say something else. Her eyes glistened. But instead, she walked stiffly to the door and returned to her spot at the front desk.

Lila dropped her head in her hands. This was the third employee they'd lost in as many months. Why did they have turnover after turnover? Was L. T. right? Was she the reason people were leaving? Lila really wished she could figure out what she was doing wrong.

A light tap on the door caused Lila to look up. Debbie, their head receptionist, stood against the frame. "Can I talk to you privately?"

Oh no. Not Debbie too. She waved her right-hand employee in. The fifty-something brilliant ball of energy who kept the office humming and could be counted on to pitch in wherever needed, entered. She filled the seat Tanya had just emptied.

"There's something you need to know. Tanya's leaving because of the way L. T. treats her."

"What do you mean?" Lila sat up straight.

"He's condescending and downright mean-spirited at times. He's that way with all of us, especially when you aren't around. He always has to be the smartest guy in the room and make sure everyone knows it." Debbie frowned. "He's an arrogant jerk."

Lila flinched at hearing one of the words she'd just told her children not to use.

"He doesn't bother me much, because I won't take his crap." Debbie paused. "Sorry to be so blunt."

Lila motioned for Debbie to continue.

"Pretty much every employee we've ever had says L. T. is creepy and makes them feel uncomfortable. The real reason you're constantly having to go through so many new hires is because of L. T."

"L. T. said employees left because of me," Lila said.

"We know," Debbie said. "But you're his wife, so no one is going to tell you how your husband really acts, especially when one of you signs our paychecks."

Lila cringed.

"But after what he did to Tanya this morning, I've had enough. Even if you fire me, it is worth it. Someone has to speak up. He made her get a small spatula and sandwich baggie from the breakroom and start scooping up cigarette butts out on the parking lot. That wasn't the worst part."

"What was the worst?"

"He stood over her the whole time. When a butt slipped off the spatula before she could get it into the baggie, he'd either laugh at her and tell her she was worthless or stupid, or he'd scream obscenities at her. I'm here to tell you, no human being deserves to be talked to like that. I know I won't take it. The first time he cusses me out, I'm gone."

Lila frowned. "Even though employees do need to be respectful and follow instructions, I cannot disagree with you that the behavior you describe is inappropriate. I'm very sorry you and the others have been treated this way. Please accept my deepest apology. I will talk to my husband tonight."

"I just thought you should know. If things don't improve around here soon, there won't be many of us left." Debbie rose from her chair. "I like you. You've always been fair. Even when you called us out, you did it professionally and you allowed people to maintain their dignity. I respect that. I respect you. But being perfectly honest? Your husband, not so much. Thanks for listening." Having said her piece, Debbie left the room.

Lila scanned the office, taking in medical certificates, association awards, community appreciation letters, and other symbols of business success for Frost & Frost Sports Medicine. Saturday, they would host their annual Sports Safety Fair, to educate athletes, coaches, and parents on best practices to prevent injuries. But as Lila considered the state of their marriage and culture of their office, she wondered how to pull it off. *How am I supposed to host this event and pretend happiness on the outside while I'm so sad on the inside? I don't want to be a fake.*

The time had come for Lila to have another serious conversation with L. T. Talking to her the way he did was one thing but teaching their children to disrespect her behind her back and driving good employees away through workplace bullying was another. Something had to change.

Lila reviewed L. T.'s patient calendar, which was easy since he only worked two and a half days a week. Lila had to pull many long days to ensure insurance billing, patient billing, accounts payables, and accounts receivables were all processed. She often went to work at 5:00 a.m., came home and got the kids off to school, and returned to the office until it was time to drive Heath to a practice, game, or other extracurricular activity. Grace also needed shuttling. At least Debbie had taken on staff scheduling.

When it came to running the business, L. T. was full of ideas. He loved developing marketing plans, creating events, and establishing fundraisers, but that was the extent of his efforts. He planned and promoted but left all implementation to Lila, without considering the reasonable amounts of time, energy, resources, and money it took to pull them off. The upcoming Sports Safety Fair was a prime example.

Yes, the annual fair was a good thing for the community, and Lila loved being able to give back in this way, but she was exhausted—mentally, emotionally, and physically. Most of her energy drain existed because she knew what was coming. She could predict with a high degree of certainty that no matter how well the sports fair succeeded, L. T. would spend the following week or two complaining about it.

Instead of focusing on appreciation for what neighbors and fellow business leaders in the community were doing to partner and participate, L. T. gossiped about them. If he couldn't identify a legitimate issue, he exaggerated or imagined a problem. Almost always, the pattern landed in the same place—L. T.'s perceived mistreatment. To hear him tell it, he was slighted by everyone.

Lila guessed correctly that L. T.'s calendar had plenty of space open. She dialed his number.

When he answered, Lila got straight to the point. "Are you finished with your workout?"

Irritated, he said, "I'm getting ready to shower."

"You need to come to the office ASAP. We need to discuss a couple of important matters."

"Can't it wait? I've got patients today."

"Mrs. Rodriguez is slated for 11:30, and Mr. Kang is coming at 1:00." Lila glanced at her watch. "It's only 10:06, so we've got time."

"Fine," L. T. groused. "Let me take my shower."

Nearly an hour later, L. T. strolled in. He prioritized neither talking with his wife nor his next patient's time. L. T. sat and Lila closed the door to her office.

"What are you fired up about this time?" he said. "I already told you I would try to keep it down in front of the kids."

Lila ignored the fresh inference that she was just a nag. She also overlooked the fact that he still did not see the urgency of changing his attitude and behavior about her, especially in front of their children. "We've got a problem here at the office."

L. T. groaned. "You see problems even when there aren't any. I think you lay in bed at night conjuring up what you can worry about the next day."

"I do not do that. I have real concerns that could cause real consequences. For you and for me, not to mention our patients."

"Well, quit circling and spit it out. What are you worried about now?"

"We lost Tanya this morning."

"So." He shrugged and crossed his legs. "She wasn't good help anyway. She didn't follow directions. I caught her drinking a soda at her station. And I know she talked about me behind my back."

Lila bristled. "We agreed the staff is allowed to have a drink and snack by their workstations, as long as they don't eat or drink in front of patients and doing so doesn't interfere with their work. And what exactly did she say about you?"

"I didn't hear what she said, but I know she talked about me. I could tell."

"So, you based your opinion on assumption and your imagination, not on something factual. We've discussed how that can get us in trouble with labor laws before."

"No one is going to convince me she wasn't talking about me. I own this place, and I'm not going to tolerate employee insubordination." He uncrossed his legs and leaned forward. "From anyone."

Lila shook her head. "Is it true you made her pick up cigarette butts with a spatula and plastic baggie? And that you stood over her and cussed her while she tried to follow those directions?"

L. T. laughed deep from his belly. "Of course that's the story you got. I didn't stand over her. Did I watch her to make sure she did the job right? Yes. But I wasn't on her back."

"And did you curse at her?"

He smirked. "I motivated her."

"So, you used profanity. You cannot do that. Our attorney told us in the eyes of the law, it's called harassment and workplace bullying. Not only are we paying for a lot of unnecessary turnover, which is expensive, but we could be sued by a disgruntled employee."

"What are you talking to our lawyer about? Why are you discussing our business behind my back?"

Lila slapped her forehead with her right palm. "I am not talking to our attorney behind your back. You were with me in her office when she reviewed labor laws. I'm just repeating what she told us then."

L. T.'s face flushed.

"And if you don't believe me, or her for that matter, google workplace harassment. There's plenty of information available online. But the point is, we cannot afford a lawsuit. And we can't keep losing good employees. We need to treat them with dignity and respect, even when we must hold them accountable." Lila leaned back in her chair. "I wouldn't mind a little dignity and respect myself. Especially when it comes to what you say about me to our kids."

L. T. stood abruptly and strode toward the door. "Here we go. It's always my fault. I'm not arguing with you anymore. I have a patient to see." He slammed the door behind him.

By the time she arrived home that night, Lila felt like she'd run into a freight train. She tried to put on a happy face in front of the kids, though she felt like a fraud by doing so. L. T. acted as if she didn't exist and focused most of his attention on Heath.

When Lila crawled into bed, L. T.'s snores reverberated through their bedroom. His peaceful face made anger rise inside her. She picked up her journal and scrawled, venting her pent-up emotions.

I'm crushed. I feel so alone. Somebody, please help me. He goes to sleep no matter what, while I lay awake trying to figure out how to make things better between us, whether we're fighting or not.

I know my Sunday school teacher always said we aren't supposed to let the sun set without settling our arguments, but I am so lost. How can I settle something with someone who is unwilling to work on our issues? How can I turn off this resentment I feel inside? I feel like I can't win, like I'm a complete failure in every part of my life. I'm worried about our children, our employees, our patients, our business, and our marriage. How can I

*make this man happy and also take care of everyone else
I'm responsible for? What am I doing wrong?*

Lila glanced at the bedside clock. 3:18 a.m. She begrudgingly
hoisted herself from bed. Since the early days of their marriage,
L. T. had refused to let her set her own alarm. He told her many
times, "I will tell you when to get up." When she needed to start
early, Lila slept fitfully, afraid of oversleeping. It would be a long
time before Lila recognized her situation for what it truly was.

FEELING WHAT YOU NEED TO FEEL

When human beings are overwhelmed with emotion because
of circumstances beyond our control, instinct wants us to shut
down our feelings. But burying the truth about our reality and
how we feel about situations turns dangerous when we become
too practiced at turning off emotions.

Numbing, ignoring, denying, and avoiding may provide
comfort in the moment, but those feelings don't disappear. They
simply hide out, waiting to bubble up. The more we bury, the
more there is to rise up and grab us—often at inopportune times.

Whether we use the support of a qualified therapist, coach,
ministry professional, or friend, ensuring we choose a sounding
board who provides healthy feedback is crucial to seeing our
challenges in a balanced way.

We should not seek allies. We should not seek detractors. We
should not seek those who will wallow with us in our misery. We
should always seek truth. If you embrace the truth, it will release
true freedom into your life. As John 8:32 says, "And you will
know the truth, and the truth will set you free" (ESV).

For a time is coming when people will no longer listen to sound and wholesome teaching. They will follow their own desires and will look for teachers who will tell them whatever their itching ears want to hear.

—2 TIMOTHY 4:3 NLT

CHAPTER FOUR

PRISON OF
Secrets and Lies

Tears shed for self are signs of weakness, but tears shed for others are a sign of strength.

—BILLY GRAHAM

*L*ila heard the knock on the front door while doing dishes. Sammy immediately barked. "Shush, Sammy," Lila said, glancing at her watch. "Who's here at 9:45 p.m.?"

She dried her hands on a red dish towel and tossed it on the counter. By the time she made it into the living room, L. T. was already opening the door.

An officer demanded, "Are you Leroy Travis Frost?"

"I am," L. T. said.

Lila gaped. Behind the officer stood several more uniformed men and women. At least four cars with swirling lights were parked haphazardly in their driveway. One had pulled onto their lawn.

The first officer said, "Turn around and place your hands behind your back."

"What's going on?" L. T. said, the panic in his voice obvious. "I haven't done anything wrong."

"Sir, you are under arrest for the solicitation of a minor, sex trafficking, confining a child for the purpose of sexual assault, sexual exploitation of a child, patronizing of a prostituted child, and assault in the first degree." The officer read L. T. his full Miranda warning and turned him toward the front door.

L. T. yelled over his shoulder. "Call a criminal attorney, Lila. Now!"

"I don't understand." Lila stammered, "You must have made a mistake."

One officer shoved L. T. into the car. Tears rolled down his face.

Tears welled up in Lila. L. T. never cried.

A woman in uniform stepped into the living room. "Ma'am your husband is being taken down to the station. I suggest you do as your husband asks and call an attorney for him. They can explain everything in detail once they review the arresting report. Here's my card." She held out a blue and black business card that read: Lieutenant Michele Stepanovich with her phone number, email, street address, and precinct number underneath.

Hands shaking, Lila accepted the card. While Lila googled "criminal attorneys near me" on her phone, the troupe of cops got in their cars and backed out. She found a listing that said a lawyer was available after business hours and clicked "Call."

Two rings in, a female voice answered.

"Please help me," Lila pleaded. "My husband has been arrested, but I think they've got the wrong person."

"Where did they take him?"

Lila steadied her hand enough to read the precinct number to the woman.

"I can be there in thirty minutes," the attorney said. "Meet me there."

"OK," Lila said. After hanging up, she took a deep breath. Thankfully, Heath and Grace were both at camp. She prayed her children never heard about what had just happened.

Lila walked into the police station and caught her breath as the thick scent of unsavory body odors and fake lavender hit her nostrils. She approached the information window timidly.

A male officer with a kind smile and warm eyes slid the window sideways. "Can I help you?"

Lila whispered, "I'm looking for information on my husband. Some policemen came to our house and arrested him."

"What's his name?"

"L. T. Frost."

"What does L. T. stand for, ma'am?"

"Oh, I'm sorry. Leroy Travis. Leroy Travis Frost is his name."

The officer clacked his keyboard. "Got him," he said. After scanning the screen, he added in a more somber tone, "You can wait over there." He pointed to a bench across the room.

Ten minutes later, the sound of a door opening made Lila turn. A medium-build, blonde woman with ruby red–rimmed glasses, lipstick to match, a dark gray tailored suit, and black pumps strode in.

Lila stood.

The woman carried herself like an attorney. She approached Lila and held out her hand in an invitation to shake. Her words tumbled out fast and confident. "I'm Maggie. Are you Lila Frost?"

"Yes," Lila said. The woman's handshake was strong, oozing with confidence and self-assurance. Lila's fingers throbbed for several seconds after they let go of each other.

"Go ahead and sit back down," Maggie said. "I'll find out what we're dealing with."

The minutes ticked with excruciating slowness while Maggie and the kind officer talked, laughed, and occasionally whispered seriously. Finally, the attorney took a seat next to Lila.

"Would you like the great news or bad first?"

Lila inhaled deeply. "It doesn't matter. I need to hear both."

"True. I'll start with the bad. Better to face it and get it over with."

Maggie's choice of wording did not comfort Lila.

"So, Leroy—"

"He actually goes by L. T. He hates his first name."

"Sorry. L. T. Anyway, he's got himself caught up in a sex trafficking investigation. Apparently, the police think they've busted a ring, and they believe your husband is part of it."

Lila gasped. "There's no way. He couldn't possibly do something like that."

Maggie patted Lila's arm with just a little too much patronizing fervor. "They say they have computer evidence and eyewitness statements, but we'll start looking into all of that tomorrow when we formalize my representation. You should be able to bond him out and take him home tonight. That's the great news."

"OK," Lila said. But nothing about this situation felt great to her.

Once everything was in motion, Maggie left. Adrenaline kept Lila awake while she waited for her husband's bail to be processed. It was wearing off almost five hours later when L. T. was escorted into the lobby. She rushed toward him. "Are you OK?" She attempted a hug, but he shrugged her off.

"I just want to go home and climb into my own bed."

"Sure," Lila said.

He didn't thank her for supporting him, and they drove home in silence.

After some restless catnapping for a few hours, Lila got up at 7:00, contacted the office staff, and asked them to call patients and reschedule appointments. Then she dialed Maggie to see what time they could meet. They agreed on 1:30 p.m., so Maggie could do prep work before L. T. and Lila arrived. When they hung up, Lila sat at the dining room table and absently watched a pair of blue jays bicker while she nursed a cup of tea. She barely noticed when it turned from lukewarm to cold. Her thoughts were too far away.

Lila reflected back on her honeymoon in Barbados. L. T.'s parents weren't wealthy, but they weren't poor either. The trip was a gift from them. On the third night, L. T. was drinking his fourth Ragged Point cocktail, a local blend of rum, apple juice, lime, sugar, and fresh ginger. He rarely consumed alcohol, so his body reacted fast.

Slurring his words, L. T. pointed to a girl who appeared to be thirteen or fourteen years old. "She reminds me of Becky. Same body type."

"Your little sister, Becky?" Lila said.

"Yeah. She had the same curves in the same places when she was that age."

"Ooookaaay," Lila drew out the word as discomfort rose inside her.

"Since we're married now, I should confess something."

Lila's unease heightened.

L. T.'s elbow slipped off the table and he nearly fell out of his chair. He clumsily righted himself. "Becky and I were really close, and we were both curious about the opposite sex, so it was easy to explore together. I should have stopped it, but we did it anyway."

"You did what?"

"You know. Played doctor."

Lila leaned back in her chair.

"Please don't reject me." L. T. reached for her hand. "That's what Dad and Mom did. They ignored us most of the time and never showed any emotion, except anger. If they had given us more attention, I might not have gotten involved in porn and other sex stuff."

Lila's voice rose. "Porn? Other sex stuff?"

Realizing what he'd just said, L. T. snapped himself more erect in his chair. His words still slurred, but he seemed more coherent. "Don't listen to me. I think I'm drunk. I don't know what I'm talking about."

Lila felt queasy, but compassion for her husband also stirred. She imagined him as a sad little boy desperate for love. She touched his hands. "I'm sorry," Lila said. "I'm here for you. No matter what. 'Til death do us part."

L. T. glanced back toward the girl and removed his hands from Lila's. "I don't like being touched unless I'm having sex."

Lila felt bile creep up the back of her throat. "I need to use the bathroom."

"OK. I'll wait right here," L. T. said. His head dropped onto the table before she scooted her chair all the way back.

Lila took her time, trying to process what her husband had just told her. She knew it was normal for children to explore sexually, but something about what L. T. said made it seem like there might have been more with his sister.

When she returned, L. T. was passed out. Lila tugged, pulled, and begged, before she finally got him to move. Their cabana was only a short walk away following a well-lit path, but it took almost thirty minutes for her to drag him along. His six-foot-three-inch frame carried much more weight than her five-foot-six-inch body. At the edge of their bed, she let gravity take over and he collapsed diagonally across it. Lila took his shoes off and went outside.

On the patio, she created a makeshift sleeping space for herself using two bamboo chairs. Sleep wouldn't come. Hours later, Lila barely noticed the gorgeous sunrise, distracted by yet another replay of the disturbing conversation she had with her husband the night before. She tried to shake her concern.

L. T. woke up cranky. When Lila brought up their evening conversation, he said he didn't remember. After she tried to jog his memory, he shouted, "Drop it! I'm not talking about that anymore!"

And so, they didn't. Not on that trip. Not for the next several years of their marriage.

Eventually, Lila successfully pushed the memory deep into the recesses of her brain. But now, sitting alone in her kitchen, the memory refused to hide. *My husband can't be a sexual predator, can he?*

L. T. walked into the kitchen a little before 11:00 a.m. He kicked at Sammy. Lila both expected and accepted her husband's selfish behavior. She had become used to it.

Lila picked up Sammy and smoothed his curly coat. "I made an appointment with the attorney for 1:30. Do we need to discuss anything before we go?" Lila kissed the top of Sammy's head before gently placing him back on the floor.

L. T. popped the top on his can of Diet Mountain Dew. "Nope. There's nothing to talk about. I didn't do anything wrong." L. T. slurped long and loudly.

L. T.'s flat statement made Lila's nausea increase. "Shouldn't we make notes before we see Maggie?"

Wheeling around, L. T. raised his voice. "Let me handle this. Do not screw this up by jacking your jaws. I will do all the talking. You just sit there and stay quiet."

Lila nodded. She knew better than to argue. Instead, she waited a couple of minutes before getting up and walking to the bedroom. She needed a dose of supernatural strength. Lila picked up her Bible and sat in her blue wingback chair. She closed her eyes and prayed out loud. "Lord, I feel so confused. Please help me understand what's true and what isn't. Tell me what to do, and please make it clear. In Jesus's name. Amen."

Lila opened her Bible to pick up where she'd left off the day before in Exodus. She started with chapter 14. When she got to verse 14, she stopped. It simply said, "The LORD will fight for you; you need only to be still."

Lila read and repeated that message to herself a number of times. It felt like a message from God. Not only did it help her now, but she would also need that comfort in the future.

BE STILL AND KNOW

In the twenty-first century, some mock faith in an unseen God. However, when life kicks us in the gut and we can't make sense of the senseless, our hope is found in Christ alone. We can confidently put our trust in the Master of the universe, who loves us deeply and defends us powerfully.

If we are hungry for wisdom and thirsty for truth to guide us, God will speak to us through the Bible. Sometimes He tells us to fight, sometimes He tells us to let Him handle everything.

One of the most difficult Scriptures in all the Bible is Psalm 46:10, where we are told to be still and know God is God. Exodus 14:14 is similarly challenging. And yet, when we stop trying to control, fix, and change our circumstances, but instead, take them to God, we find relief.

The answers may not come as quickly as we would like, but with perseverance, resolve, and unwavering faith, we will ultimately find the deliverance we seek. God's love and provision can help us overcome any fear—even when the form it arrives in isn't what we expected.

For the Lord will go before you,
the God of Israel will be your rear guard.

—ISAIAH 52:12

CHAPTER FIVE

TECHNICALITIES

A half-truth is a whole lie.

—YIDDISH PROVERB

*L*ila dutifully followed L. T. into the attorney's office. She grabbed the door before it swung shut in her face. Why couldn't he be bothered to hold the door for her?

Maggie raised a dark brown chiseled eyebrow when they entered. "You must be Leroy," Maggie said.

"L. T."

"Pardon me. I stand corrected. L. T. it is," Maggie said. "Have a seat."

Maggie extended a hand to Lila and with a softer tone said, "Nice to see you again."

"Thank you," Lila said quietly, afraid to add anything more. She didn't want to make L. T. mad.

L. T. leaned forward in his chair and got straight to the point. "Can you get me off?"

Maggie's piercing stare indicated she could not be intimidated. "Your charges are serious, Mr. Frost. And they do have evidence—"

"What evidence? I didn't do anything wrong!" L. T. pounded the attorney's desk.

Lila flinched and pulled the sleeves of her sweater over her hands.

"Calm down, Mr. Frost. Getting emotional isn't going to help your case."

"You try being brought up on bogus charges and tell me how unemotional you are."

Maggie pushed the nosepiece of her ruby red glasses in place with an index finger sporting glazed polish. She kept her eyes squarely on L. T. "Since I'm not the one who was arrested last night, you might want to listen. If you will let me finish, we can move on to strategy."

"Fine." L. T. pushed himself back in his chair.

Maggie folded her hands together on the top of her desk. "They have computer evidence and eyewitness statements according to documents on file. However, I'll dig deeper to determine exactly how they gathered their evidence. It might take me and my team several days, but I'll know more by your arraignment." Maggie stopped and clicked something on her computer. "That hearing is scheduled for June 29."

"That's almost two months away. I want to get this over with. They can't prove I did anything wrong." L. T. huffed. "And I see patients on Wednesdays."

Lila took note of the subtle change in L. T.'s verbiage to "They can't prove I did anything wrong."

"You'll never hear anyone say the wheels of justice turn fast," Maggie said. "But remember, we need time to build our case, just like the prosecutor does. It's to our advantage to adequately prepare." Maggie's lips tightened. "And as far as your priorities are concerned, this case just took over your life. The courts don't care what you have on your calendar, they set dates for hearings, and we are required to show up."

"Great," L. T. said.

"If we request a continuance," Maggie said, "we'd better have excellent cause. Judges don't like unnecessary delays that inconvenience them and cost taxpayers more money. However, if the court wants to postpone, that's at their whim, and we have no choice but to acquiesce. I suggest you reschedule your Wednesday patients."

"What a bunch of bull." L. T. slapped a hand on his leg.

"Call it what you will, but serious charges have been leveled against you." Maggie picked up her phone and read, scanning line by line with a ruby nail. "Solicitation of a minor, sex trafficking, confining a child for the purpose of sexual assault, sexual exploitation of a child, patronizing of a prostituted child, and assault first degree." She looked at L. T. "These are not the kinds of accusations you want to disregard or take lightly. We have a lot of work to do." She turned toward Lila. "Mrs. Frost, do you have any questions?"

Lila shook her head.

After they signed the formal agreement and wrote a $15,000 check for the attorney's retainer, L. T. and Lila left the office in silence. When they got in the car, Lila wrung her hands and didn't stop for the entirety of the drive, even while L. T. talked.

"You know I didn't do any of the things they are accusing me of, right?"

"I know," Lila said. But she secretly wondered what she should believe. On one hand, the police officers took her husband away in handcuffs and sounded certain about the charges. L. T. had his faults, but she did too. On the other, she wanted to believe her husband.

Over the next seven weeks, Lila tried to occupy her mind with work, kids, and other activities. But the dark cloud of foreboding followed her everywhere. June 25, Maggie called and asked if she and L. T. could meet right away.

In the office, Maggie said, "Dr. Frost, you are a lucky man. The purported witnesses in your case have substantially changed their stories and are refusing to cooperate with the prosecuting attorney. It also seems a necessary warrant was not filed prior to law enforcement's seizure of computers and other electronic devices that held emails and text messages, some of which you are reported to be a party. Therefore, the prosecutor does not have sufficient evidence and the case is being dropped."

L. T. stood. "Ha! I told you."

Maggie stood as well. "I understand your celebratory mood, Dr. Frost. However, I must caution you. Be assured that you are on the radar of law enforcement now. They will watch you for a very long time. If you truly want this to be over, don't make a misstep."

"Got it," L. T. said haughtily. "Let's go, Lila. I want to play some golf."

Maggie came around her desk and touched Lila lightly on the arm. "If you ever need anything, you've got my number."

"I appreciate it," Lila said, barely making eye contact.

On the sidewalk outside the building, L. T. turned to his wife and demanded, "What was that about? Why did she tell you to call if you ever needed anything?"

"I honestly don't know."

"Well, we won't need her anymore. Right?"

Lila recognized the tinge of threat in L. T.'s tone. "I can't imagine why we would. I'm sure she was just being nice."

Minutes later, L. T. dropped Lila off at the office and headed to the golf course, his demeanor a cross between lighthearted and smug. Lila didn't share his level of enthusiasm.

In the ensuing years, anytime Lila raised concerns or fears of any kind regarding L. T.'s behaviors, he referenced this arrest and release. No matter how gentle her approach or cushioned her questions, he squelched her voice with one standing statement. "Stop attacking me. People smarter than you have tried to bring me down and look where that got them. Stop being stupid."

Without fail, his manipulation did its job and brought Lila's voice of fear to life. Her self-esteem fell as her inner doubts rose. Over time, Lila developed distrust in her ability to assess truth from fiction. It was easier to let the sleeping bear lie. Years later however, Lila was finally forced to open her eyes.

WHERE GROWTH BEGINS

Fighting back lying voices that fuel our fears requires intentionality, consistent courage, and energy, whether they originate from our own minds or the words of others. Life is a constant balancing act between pushing ourselves and giving ourselves grace. Courageous change cannot occur if we do not first identify and accept truth—often a truth right in front of our eyes that we continually attempt to deny.

Life is a series of choices, and no one will get 100 percent of their decisions right. But we would do well to follow the standard of legendary UCLA basketball coach John Wooden: "The true test of a man's character is what he does when no one is watching."

Real growth begins where others can't see. What we do when people are watching is not as significant as our resolve to act with integrity when we believe we are alone.

Is there a hard truth you are denying? Open your mind and accept it. Is there a fearful voice keeping you cowering? Decide to stand up to it/them and develop a strategy to act against forces bent on holding you back.

Do you want to transform your fear into faith? Start privately and quietly, in that place between you and God where no one else knows. Read your Bible. Pray. Seek His guidance. Speak gratitude instead of anxiety.

God is on your side, even when you don't see or feel Him. He's working on your behalf, even when it feels like all hope is lost. He's willing to provide clarity, even if it takes a while for you to see what He's trying to show you. He knows your true value, even when you don't see it in yourself.

Be strong and courageous. Do not be afraid or terrified because of them, for the LORD your God goes with you; he will never leave you nor forsake you.

—DEUTERONOMY 31:6

CHAPTER SIX

LEAD *Up*

Life is 10 percent what happens to you and 90 percent how you react to it.

—CHARLES SWINDOLL

*L*ila walked out of Grant's counseling office and winced when a flash of lightning stabbed the steel-gray horizon. A crack of thunder echoed seconds later. She hustled toward the parking lot and her car, hoping to beat the rain.

A drop plopped onto Lila's shoulder as she pulled her keys from her purse. She fumbled to grip the key fob when her phone rang. "Ugh," she groaned and reached for the phone. It slipped from Lila's fingers. She tried to grab it with her other hand and ended up in a quick game of hot potato. By the time she had a handle on both phone and fob, a torrent pummeled her from overhead. And yet, the phone kept ringing.

Lila unlocked her car door and ducked inside. She turned the phone to read the display and wondered what was wrong now.

When she answered, L. T. demanded, "What are you doing?"

"Trying to get dry at the moment. But I just left my counseling appointment."

"I still don't see why you think you need a therapist." L. T. didn't like the inability to control what "personal business" Lila shared.

"It's something I need for me."

"Great," L. T. said sarcastically. He was midstream in his sentence when Lila's phone connected to the car's Bluetooth. "I'll be late tonight. I've got that patient health class lecture after work."

"I remember."

"Also, I talked Heath into seeing a counselor. I made an appointment for us tomorrow."

It didn't escape Lila's notice that L. T. had no issue with their son seeing someone.

"What time? I've got back-to-back patients from 10:30 in the morning until 1:00, so if we need to be there in that time slot, it's going to interfere with my calendar."

"Oh, you don't need to worry about going. I'll handle it."

Lila bit her bottom lip. "You made the appointment, you're going to take him, and you're going to attend the session with him?" Lila knew L. T. only wanted to go with Heath to shape the narrative.

"Yep. You said you wanted me to play a more active parenting role."

"I did, but—"

"I thought this would make you happy. I'm doing what you asked."

Lila knew she should feel pleased, so why did she feel agitated and confused? Something in her gut recognized danger, but she couldn't pinpoint what was bothering her. "OK, I guess."

"See you tonight."

After the call ended, Lila held on to the steering wheel for several minutes while rain pelted the windshield. She hated feeling so afraid without understanding why.

That night, L. T. came home even later than normal from giving his lecture, walking in the door at 8:15 p.m.

Lila tried to keep the tension she felt out of her voice. "What kept you so long?"

"I had a patient who asked a lot of questions. I stayed after to talk with him once everyone else left."

Strange. You normally make excuses, so you don't have to talk with patients longer than necessary. She dared say none of this aloud.

L. T. yawned and stretched his hands over his head. "I'm beat. I'm going to bed."

"Already?"

"Yeah. I told you I was beat."

Lila did not receive a goodnight kiss or other demonstrations of affection. She heard L. T. stop and say good night to Heath. By his footsteps, she could tell he didn't bother checking on Grace.

The next day, Lila walked into the kitchen and was surprised to see her husband already awake.

In a syrupy sweet tone, L. T. said, "Would you like me to fix your tea?"

"Uh, no. That's OK. I can fix it myself."

"Suit yourself."

Lila wrinkled her forehead. "What's up with you? Why are you offering to make me something to drink?"

"Can't a husband do something nice for his wife?" L. T. smiled.

"You never do nice things for me," Lila said without thinking.

A splotch of red immediately raised on L. T.'s neck, and Lila steeled herself. But he surprised her by taking a long breath before speaking. "I love you, babe. I'll see you tonight." He walked over, kissed her forehead, and disappeared out the door.

Lila frowned. *Where is this behavior coming from?*

But that evening, L. T.'s mood swung 180 degrees. When Lila entered their living room after a long day of treating patients and office administration, she saw L. T. sprawled on the couch. He opened his eyes ever so slightly when the door shut.

"What do you want for dinner?" she said.

"Can't you see I'm resting? Do not disturb me."

Lila and the kids tried not to make any noise the rest of the night. After baths, Grace complained that her tummy hurt. As soon as he heard her say it, L. T. perked up. "Come on pumpkin, I'll go lay down with you. We can watch a movie."

Confused again, partially from his kindness, but also because L. T. rarely spent time with Grace, Lila protested. "It's a school night."

"There's just no pleasing you."

L. T. was still emotionally cold the following morning. He scooted Sammy out of his path roughly with his foot and didn't speak directly to Lila while she fixed her breakfast of boiled eggs, turkey bacon, and avocado toast. But beneath his breath she heard him say, "No wonder you're getting a belly and back fat."

Tears blurred Lila's vision as she scooped two slices of bacon onto her plate. "Why do you do that to me?"

"What?"

"Make comments about my weight. You know that's a sensitive subject for me. I heard what you said."

"There you go making something out of nothing. I just noticed you're getting a little thicker in the middle, that's all. But look, you're fine for me. Don't you want me to help you?"

Lila was tiring of L. T.'s condescending way of pointing out her flaws, but then acting like he was a martyr who tolerated her imperfections. She knew the pattern and now saw through his attempts to make her feel bad about herself. He wasn't the first person to make her feel "less than" as a human being.

During her teenaged years, friends told Lila how athletic she looked, but when she viewed herself in the mirror, she saw an obese person. The words of her paternal grandmother always echoed in her mind. "You're getting a little belly on you. You might want to stick with the diet food I'm eating."

Throughout high school and college, Lila's deep dislike for herself caused her to obsessively step on the scale. Where she never saw weight issues on others, she saw them constantly on herself. In college, Lila tried different diets to slim down. She limited her diet to twelve hundred calories per day, she tried eliminating all fat, and she restricted her meat intake. Lila's constant hunger caused her weight to fluctuate and led to a cycle of starving and bingeing.

During Lila's pregnancy with Heath, her body sensitivity made her feel obese in the first trimester, before her baby bump even showed. She was so small, multiple people questioned whether Lila was truly pregnant or not. She gained only fifteen pounds during her entire pregnancy. When her doctor told her she needed to gain weight, Lila finally accepted that she wasn't truly fat. She successfully drowned out the ever-critical echo of her grandmother's voice. Learning to stop those old messages gave Lila a first taste of standing up for herself.

But L. T. was like kryptonite for Lila's inner strength—he weakened her emotionally and mentally. His off-balancing comments made her grandmother's criticism seem like compliments. This morning was no exception.

When L. T. left, Lila pushed her plate aside. She fed on memories instead of food, thinking back to her senior year of high school. The year her father walked out without any notice.

After he left, day after day, her dad drove past their house on his way to the home of his mistress and her children. He rarely stopped. Even worse was seeing him drive the other woman's kids around as if they were his. He'd traded his old family in for a new one. Lila's mother showed no emotion and refused to talk about it. Eventually, that decision caught up with her.

When Lila's mom became depressed and stopped preparing meals or caring where her daughter was or what she did, Lila stepped up and fended for herself. The stress made Lila's mom either lose sight of her eldest daughter and forget she existed or falsely believe Lila didn't need affection or attention. Lila took on the responsibility of both mother and father, until her mom eventually sought help and got her life back in order.

Lila also lost her favorite uncle, Vern, during her senior year. His care and kindness comforted her after her parents' split. But even more so, Uncle Vern made Lila feel acceptable for who she was. He was like the loving father she didn't have. He didn't call her derogatory names. He didn't make digs about her personality. He loved her without trying to alter her in any way.

But Uncle Vern died in a car accident. He had called to check on her that same morning. By the time school let out, Uncle Vern was gone. And took a lot of Lila's self-esteem with him.

Lila had known for decades that the sudden absence of these three important adult relationships—father, mother, and uncle—was the source of her abandonment issues. It was one of the biggest reasons she tolerated so much from L. T. and kept trying to please him. She also did not want her children to feel the loss of a parent like she had. And so again, as she sat in her kitchen, Lila decided to stay.

By lunch, it seemed Lila's commitment to her marriage was well-founded, odd and stressful as things were.

Lila was updating computer records when a light tap sounded on her door. "Come in."

L. T. singsonged his way in. "Hey, honey. What's up?"

Lila stopped and wondered who had invaded her husband this time. "I'm trying to finish this reconciliation."

L. T. came around the desk and massaged her shoulders.

Lila stiffened ever so slightly. He never touched her unless he wanted sex. Though he had a voracious sensual appetite, even then his physical contact was about gratifying himself, never for Lila's pleasure or satisfaction.

L. T. kissed the top of her head and pulled her hands off the computer keyboard. "You work too hard."

Lila allowed her husband to guide her to a standing position. She wondered how he could be so mean in the morning and so thoughtful a few hours later. This would not be the last time she pondered that type of question for the day. She did, however, give in when his advances turned sexual—as usual. It felt good to be wanted, if only for a few minutes.

That evening, Lila ordered Chinese takeout for supper, since they had the kids' back-to-school night to attend. Apparently, L. T. forgot.

"Are you kidding? That's tonight? I need to work out."

"But Daddy" Grace pleaded, "I want you to see my room and meet my teacher. All the kids' parents will be there."

"Fine," L. T. threw his napkin on the table. "I'll take a shower."

After he stomped out of the room, Lila thought she heard his muffled voice talking to someone. But his cell phone still lay on the counter where he'd left it. Weird.

Grace whispered, "Why is Dad mad."

"You know how he is about his workouts." Lila tried to downplay with a forced chuckle.

Laughing, Heath added, "And his sleep."

"And his sleep." Lila chuckled again.

When they arrived at the school, L. T. greeted acquaintances like long-lost family, completely shifting his personality again.

Grace tugged Lila's hand and dragged her down the hall to her classroom. After chatting with the teacher for about fifteen minutes, she let Grace socialize with some of her classmates so she could go find L. T.

It didn't take long for her to find him. He stood in the midst of a group of people telling a story in a louder than normal voice.

"Yeah, I had to show the wife how it was done. No wonder she kept slicing. If the wife listened to me more often, she'd probably shave at least four strokes off her game."

One of the men listening shuffled his feet uncomfortably. "Hey, Lila, great to see you."

Her face flush, Lila returned the greeting.

L. T. didn't even have the decency to pretend embarrassment. He continued with his story as if Lila wasn't there.

After the kids were in bed, Lila asked L. T., "Why did you refer to me as 'the wife' to the Johnsons?"

"I always call you that when I'm talking to people."

"Why would you not use my name?"

"Well, you are my wife, aren't you? Don't you think you're being petty?"

"I think you're being disrespectful."

"You would. Just drop it. I'm done talking about this. I'm changing into my gym clothes. Don't wait up."

After he left, Lila closed her bedroom door behind her. It was time to investigate.

She rummaged through L. T.'s jackets and pants pockets until sweat formed on her neck. Nothing. She dug some more until she spotted a dark green gym bag in the back corner of the closet under a pair of L. T.'s shoes.

Lila pulled it into the light and unzipped the top. She found nothing unusual inside. But when she picked up the bag to place it where she found it, Lila felt a hard bulge in a side pocket. She stuck her hand in and drew out a cell phone.

L. T. had a phone she didn't know about.

ACKNOWLEDGING REALITY

Some women don't know what they don't know about being controlled, bullied, abused, betrayed, and treated cruelly. They also haven't made the connection between current events and their own historical experiences. The key to unlocking our freedom in current situations is to take the courageous step of facing fears and events from our yesterdays.

It is nearly impossible to find our way to happiness without analyzing how the things we've been through are connected to what we're going through. We must accept the impact of previous events on our lives. And further healing takes place when we assess the positives along with the negatives from our past. Some days are bad, but there's still good in every day.

Within our hurtful moments, if we search deeply through the rubble, we will identify moments that humbled and strengthened us. We are who we are because of what we've learned. And when we face down the voices of fear holding us back, take courage, and embrace our real value as defined by God, we can discover the key to lasting joy.

So if the Son sets you free,
you will be free indeed.

—JOHN 8:36

CHAPTER SEVEN

THE BIG
Announcement

No matter what has happened to you in the past or what is going on in your life right now, it has no power to keep you from having an amazingly good future if you will walk by faith in God.

—JOYCE MEYER

*L*ila waited in the living room for her husband to come home from the gym. L. T. walked in the door at 10:35 p.m. and she immediately confronted him with the extra cell phone. "What is this? Why do you have another phone?"

L. T. looked at Lila curiously for several seconds. "You're so nosy. If you must know, I got it to plan your surprise birthday party. As usual, though, you ruin anything I try to do for you."

"Why do you need a different device to plan a party? I don't go through your phone; I never have. But maybe I should start."

L. T. stepped toward Lila. A menacing grimace crossed his face. "Don't threaten me. It's not my fault you have to stick your nose where it doesn't belong." His attitude shifted in a heartbeat. All his features and body language softened. "Look, babe, I don't want to fight with you. I just wanted you to have the best birthday ever. I wanted you to know how much I appreciate you and all you do. Now, I'm tired. Can we please get some sleep?"

Stunned by the switch, Lila didn't know what to say.

L. T. snatched the phone from her hand and walked out of the room.

Throughout the night, Lila flipped from side to side for hours, as sleep again eluded her. Too many questions ran through her head, too many things did not add up. Lila made a mental note to talk to Grant, her counselor, about L. T.'s strange behavior over the past week. She also wanted to discuss the buried memories bubbling up.

At her Friday session, Lila spoke faster than normal, trying to make sure she got everything out and not wanting to waste Grant's time. When she finished blurting out all that was on her mind, Lila pleaded, "Am I crazy? L. T. says I make mountains out of molehills and exaggerate reality. Am I doing that?"

Grant's tone was warm and encouraging. "Have you exaggerated? When you analyze your past with absolute honesty, do you see any areas where you overdramatized the events you experienced? Have you made anything out to be more than what you authentically recall?"

"No," Lila said meekly.

"OK. Is what you've told me about L. T.'s recent behaviors accurate? Have you embellished or added more to the accounts than what you've told me?"

"No. I'm sure my memory isn't perfect, but I've tried to tell you exactly what he said, what I said, and what took place. No more and no less."

Grant leaned forward in his chair. "If you are so careful to relate things accurately, why do you think you allow someone else's questions to make you question yourself? Why do you take on guilt for conflicts, regardless of their origin?"

"I guess because I've been blamed for so much in my life."

"And is it possible you've felt abandoned by those you should have been able to trust most? In an effort to please them and keep them from leaving, do you accept unhealthy guilt so they will stay and won't be upset with you? Is it possible this is a coping skill you've developed to try and control situations that scare you and make you feel helpless?"

Lila laughed nervously. "Wow, you know how to get in my head."

Grant smiled. "I'd like you to think on the things we've talked about after you leave today. Journal your thoughts. Don't worry about making sense, don't try to write neatly or type in perfect sentences. Just get the heart of your emotions out. The act of digging down to the truth of how we feel can provide a lot of clarity and become a catalyst for deeper healing."

"I can do that."

"Great. Our time's up, but we'll talk about this more in our next session. OK?"

"OK." Lila stood, noticing she felt a little lighter and slightly more confident than when she'd walked in the door. Before going to work, Lila decided to make a pit stop.

She pulled into her accountant's office twelve minutes later and approached the receptionist. "I don't have an appointment, but is Cal available?"

"I can check." The receptionist picked up the phone and punched a number. "Can you see Dr. Lila Frost?" She laid the phone in its cradle and smiled. "Go on back."

Without exchanging pleasantries, Lila spoke directly. "Could I use your computer to take care of an important personal matter?"

Cal furrowed his brow. "I guess. Is your computer broken?"

"No. But I have a feeling I need to make sure I don't use either my work or home computer for this. I'm not even sure why I feel this way."

Cal stood and stepped away from his desk. "It's all yours. You're not doing anything illegal or inappropriate, are you?"

"You know me better than that." Lila opened a note on her phone and typed the domain name written there into the computer. "I just feel like I need to take care of this today."

Cal put his hands up in mock protest. "See no evil, hear no evil. I'll leave you to it."

Lila logged in to her insurance company profile and clicked around until she found the right form. She changed a name, downloaded the updated document, hit print, and signed it. "Do you have a scanner?" Lila looked at Cal.

"Yep," Cal said. "Do you want to email it somewhere or just save it?"

"I'm changing my life insurance beneficiary from L. T. to my mom. I want to make sure she gets my benefits in case something happens to me. I'm going to email this, but I also want to snail mail a print copy. Can you take care of mailing it for me?"

"Is something going on between you and L. T.?"

"Not necessarily. But I have this sense I need to take measures, just in case. So, will you mail this today?"

Cal looked concerned. "I can."

"Today. Not tomorrow?"

"I'll get it in today's mail."

Lila hit send to email the digital form and stood. "This is important."

"Got it."

Lila gave him a quick hug and sprinted out the door. She went to the office and pretended everything was normal for the rest of the day.

At 6:30 p.m., Lila walked into her kitchen. She wanted to journal before starting supper. A couple of points had come up in her counseling session, and she'd waited all day to document them.

She was surprised to see L. T. sitting at the table, obviously waiting for her. He had left the office late in the morning and later called to say he had to run important errands. He asked when she would be home and told her he'd see her after his workout. But she didn't expect him this early.

"I took the kids to hang out with their friends." He motioned for her to sit. "Have a seat, I made dinner."

As Lila sat, she noted the two paper plates across from each other with two slices of pizza on each. She wasn't typically welcomed home with dinner and a kind greeting. This was odd. She and L. T. hadn't even been on a date in over five years. And now he's making dinner. Lila glanced around the kitchen. "Where's Sammy?"

"I put him in our bedroom so he wouldn't bother us."

"You never let him—"

"We need to talk."

Lila's stomach felt like someone dropped a heavy stone inside it. Her appetite vanished.

"How was your counseling appointment today?"

Lila's heart quickened. L. T. must have something specific in mind. "It went well. Why?"

"Good," L. T. said. "What did you and Grant talk about?"

"Just my feelings."

"Did you tell him about getting mad at me because I took everyone to Ruby Tuesday without asking your opinion the other day?"

Lila knew he'd somehow found her private journal hidden in the laundry room and read it. The day of the Ruby Tuesday incident, L. T. had screamed at Lila and called her names. All because she'd said it would be nice if he considered her feelings by asking where she wanted to eat sometime. After he'd stopped yelling, Lila kept silent and cried quietly. At the restaurant, she barely touched her food.

L. T. pounded the table and pulled Lila back to the present. "Are you seeing someone?"

"No! Why would you say that?"

"I think you're gay and you're having an affair with a woman. I know you are doing stuff with women when you stay out late with your girlfriends."

Lila was appalled. Don't take the bait, she reminded herself. She focused on speaking slowly and calmly. "First, the only time I've stayed out late was over ten years ago. I wouldn't dare do it again because of how you overreacted then, and you've never let me forget it since. I didn't know chatting at a coffee shop until 11:00 p.m. was a federal crime. I cannot recall the last time I hung out with a friend since."

Shouting, L. T. said, "What did you do with her?"

"Ten years ago?" Lila asked, hardly able to digest why he was bringing this up now. "Nothing."

"I know you're gay because I heard Marlene that night in our driveway. She told you she loved you." L. T. sniffed. "That's not normal."

"You mean when my best friend said she loved me as she expressed frustration because you hardly let me talk to her, much less see her, because you wanted to keep me all to yourself?" Lila hung her head, took a deep breath, and looked back up at L. T. "I lost that friendship because you browbeat me."

"I think we can agree that we've both been extremely miserable for the past three years." He lowered his tone slightly. "Actually, strike that. We've been miserably unhappy for at least ten years."

"I'm not miserable," Lila said. "I mean, could things improve between us? Of course. But after sixteen years, you expect some distance and to have to work harder."

"It's more than that. We've both been unhappy for a decade."

"I can't believe you're telling me this." Lila sighed.

"I stayed for the kids." L. T. interlocked his fingers and placed his hands on the table. "But we need to separate now."

"Separate? Do I have any say-so in this?"

"Look, I've made up my mind. You can go home and see your family. The kids and I need a break from you anyway."

"Our kids? I'm not leaving, and I'm certainly not going anywhere without my children."

"*Our* children need protection." L. T. sneered. "Don't try to fight me on this. You will lose. I promise. I've already talked to Heath's counselor, and she agrees with me. It's best if the kids get a break from your mental abuse."

"*My* mental abuse? My *abuse*? I'm not the one that causes everyone else in the household to walk on eggshells. L. T., I'm begging you, don't do this!"

"Heath and Grace both want to live with me, and they want you to move out." L. T. gobbled a slice of his pizza.

"You talked to our children without me? You told our kids you wanted to separate before you told me?"

"Heath hates you. Grace is sad because of you. They're both scared all the time. They're afraid you're going to hurt them."

"Because you yell so much," Lila said. "They're afraid because they never know which Dad they're going to get from moment to moment—mad Dad or glad Dad. Frankly, I know how they feel. You tell Grace that if she doesn't go along with what you tell her you are going to knock her teeth out."

"I found a bunch of pornography on our computers, nudes of women, and I know you're seeing someone else," he said. "I also had someone check and you've taken money out of our accounts." L. T. took another bite of pizza.

Lila felt the air whoosh out of her lungs, as if someone had sucker punched her in the gut. After she caught her breath, she said, "You know you're the one looking at pornography. You're the one hiding another phone. Are *you* having an affair?"

L. T. chuckled. "I wish."

"And you know I track our money down to the penny in our accounting software. Every account we have is reconciled and matches our bank statements. For years, I tried to get you to sit down and let me go over our income and expenses with you, but you refused."

"That's not how I see it," L. T. said. "I asked you to review our finances on Sunday."

Lila sucked in a deep breath. "Look, whatever problems we have, they're solvable if we work together. I have been faithful. I have not taken any money. I cut our biweekly paychecks—and mine is exactly the same as yours. All our income is deposited into our joint accounts. And if I need to work on being a better mom, I will do whatever it takes."

"It's too late, Lila. I'm done. It's over. I want a divorce. One of us is going to be gone by tomorrow. I've decided. The kids and I want you out of the house right away."

Lila smacked the table. "You decided? I am not leaving. You will not accuse me of abandoning our children."

"I've already seen an attorney. He's practiced for over twenty years and knows how to handle difficult divorce cases. He said it's better if we separate first and try to work things out amicably between us. It will be easier on the kids and our finances. I'm trying to help you."

"Help me? I've been seeing a counselor to work on myself, while you've been seeing an attorney and planning our divorce behind my back. You refused to stop doing pornography all these years. You even put a date rape drug in my drink and posted nude pictures of me all over the internet. You wrote disgusting things to other men and women in chat rooms pretending to be me. You've isolated me and convinced me I was the problem."

L. T. grinned. "What proof do you have? None, that's what. If you want to fight me, go ahead; it won't make a difference. Do what I'm telling you. You need to go to your mom's for a couple of days, or maybe a couple of weeks, visit with your dying grandfather. I can't believe he has hung on for this long. I'll file for our legal separation, so you won't have to mess with it."

Lila stood and stiffened her back. "I'm not doing that."

"Talk about controlling. Look at you." He stood and grinned. "Have it your way. I'm going to the office."

L. T. walked away and left Lila at the kitchen table—to cry and hyperventilate.

GETTING THROUGH

Life and other people do not always play according to our rules or expectations. When life blindsides us, we are often temporarily sidelined as we struggle to process the nightmare that we wish we could wake up from.

Grief comes in many forms. We certainly mourn the death of a loved one, but we also grieve the loss of jobs, opportunities, finances, health, and relationships. Anything that shakes our peace can make us feel as if the world has spun out of control.

We wonder how to regain our bearings when we weren't offered a choice in circumstances beyond our influence. When the unimaginable strikes, we want everything righted—now.

But healing rarely happens dramatically or quickly. Restoring peace usually occurs in imperceptible moments of progress: gripping God's hand and taking one tiny step forward, and one more after it, and one more again, until those small efforts carry us to a better place. Holding on and taking one second at a time when we're too overwhelmed to do anything more. It's only when we look back that we see how far we've come and realize we were stronger than we knew.

The LORD is a shelter for the oppressed,
a refuge in times of trouble.
Those who know your name trust in you,
for you, O LORD, do not abandon those who
search for you.

—PSALM 9:9–10 NLT

CHAPTER EIGHT

RISING

Some days there won't be a song in your heart. Sing anyway.

—EMORY AUSTIN

*T*he next day, Lila poured herself into work, trying to avoid her own thoughts and emotions and thankful that L. T. had the day off. She locked the door to the office at 8:42 p.m. Although physically beat, she felt mentally and emotionally stronger than she had earlier. At least her patients appreciated her. However, a few good hours did not mean the difficulties were over.

When Lila pulled into her driveway, she saw L. T.'s Corvette in the garage, even though no lights shone in the house. She walked to the door leading into the house and tried the doorknob. It turned, meaning he was home. Lila cautiously pushed the door open, and her pulse quickened.

Inside, she moved through the dark and eerily silent house. Sammy wasn't even there to greet her. She double-checked her watch. 9:07 p.m. Too early for everyone to be in bed.

Lila passed through the dark and quiet living room. Weird.

Lila crept up the steps, illuminated only by small nightlights. About midway, she heard muffled voices.

As Lila crested and entered the second floor, she glanced toward Heath's room. No narrow strip of yellow-white beamed beneath his door. Her son was either gone or asleep at an unusually early hour.

The voices Lila heard were now louder, and she could tell they emanated from the television in her bedroom where L. T. watched his favorite murder mystery. She hoped he wasn't looking for ideas.

Practicing a fortitude exercise Grant had taught her, Lila took a cleansing breath and let it out slowly. She walked quietly to the closed door, placed her hand on the doorknob, and turned. Locked. She jiggled the knob.

The television went silent "Who's there?" L. T. shouted.

"Your wife. Who do you think it is? Let me in."

"I told you that me and the kids want you out."

"This is my house too."

"You are not sleeping in here."

Lila sighed. "At least let me have my toothbrush."

Lila stepped back at a sound inside the room. She just wanted to grab her toothbrush, toothpaste, and underwear for work the next day, then she'd go sleep downstairs. She had some extra clothes in the guest room closet.

Instead she heard a scraping sound. Seriously? He was moving the chest of drawers in front of their door?

Lila raised her voice a decibel. "Let me have my toothbrush. And where are the kids?"

"You need to leave. Now."

Lila strode to her office and pulled the desk drawer open. She removed a large paperclip. Lila went back to the master bedroom and tried jimmying the lock. The clip snapped in two.

"What are you doing?" L. T. asked. "Just give up."

"Tell me where my children are and let me get my stuff so I can brush my teeth and I'll leave."

"You'll go?" L. T. said. "You promise?"

"Fine. I promise."

The sliding sound resumed. When it stopped, the lock clicked. L. T. inched the door open and stood behind it as if scared Lila would attack him.

"Ridiculous," Lila whispered and breezed past him toward the master bath. "Where are Heath and Grace?" Lila grabbed her toiletries.

"Heath is at Rob's and Grace is with Sadie. They needed a break from all your stress."

"I did not create this situation. Any stress originated with you." Lila strode to her dresser drawer. "And where is Sammy? Why isn't he in the kitchen?"

"You are such a !@#$%," L. T. said. He lowered his voice. "I should beat the snot out of you."

Eyes wide, Lila turned to face her husband. L. T. had never struck her before, but he had pushed her against a wall, knocked her arm off a desk, and threatened to hit her many times. She always felt like he was one emotional snap away from unleashing his darker side on her.

"Please, I don't want to argue. I just need a couple of personal things." Lila inched backwards toward the door.

L. T. stepped closer until their bodies almost touched. He towered over Lila and sneered down at her, his breathing coming in snorts, like a bull ready to fight. When he spoke, it sounded more like a whispered growl. "I really should just beat the snot out of you."

The panic in Lila rose to terror level. He might act on his words this time. But she willed herself to stand strong, despite her fear. "I'm done here. I got what I needed. Please just let me go."

He leaned back without taking a step and mumbled, "This is exactly why you are such a !@#$%. Get out of here. I'm tired and want to go to sleep."

Lila backed away from her husband, carrying only the three items he allowed her to take. How can anyone possibly get a good night's rest in this house tonight?

As she started down the stairs, L. T. shouted, "You are a mean-spirited woman, and everyone is going to owe me an apology when they find out who you really are. Good riddance."

Lila eased down the stairwell, back straight, chin held high, focused on not showing her fear, even though all she wanted was to escape L. T.'s anger. The bedroom door slammed shut and the lock clicked again. She relaxed. And heard him slide the chest of drawers back.

The thumping of Lila's head woke her up from a groggy, half-asleep state. She picked up her phone and groaned. "It's only 2:10? You've got to be kidding."

She had woken up several times during the night, each time to avoid falling off the narrow couch cushions. Lila decided to get up and brew a cup of tea in hopes the warmth would relax some of the tension in her body.

While the water heated, Lila opened her purse and hunted for her neck massager, hoping it would relieve the tension behind her headache. Standing up to L. T. the previous night was a big step for her. Lila pulled her keys out to make room in her purse while she dug. Something caught her eye when she laid them on the kitchen table. Her house key was gone, and so was her copy of L. T.'s car key. Why?

At 5:00 o'clock, Lila heard the muted din of L. T.'s alarm.

When he stumbled into the kitchen, he scowled at Lila. "What are you doing here?"

"Having tea in *my* home," she said. "I slept on the couch, since you locked me out of our bedroom last night."

"You locked me out first."

Lila cocked her eyebrow at her husband. "I most certainly did not."

"You locked me out last Wednesday evening. I came home and tried to get into the bedroom, and you had the door locked. What were you doing in there that you didn't want me to see?"

Lila chuckled. "You mean when I was soaking in my bubble bath and didn't want the kids to walk in on me? Where are all these vain imaginations coming from?"

"I'm tired of being controlled," he said, "Especially financially. I'm going to show you what it feels like."

Lila looked at her husband curiously. "What are you talking about? I do not control you."

"You control whether I can spend money or not."

Lila swirled honey into her tea. "I admit I've had to make sure we had the money you wanted to spend before you went where you wanted or purchased whatever it was you set your eyes on. Remember when you bought the boat and I had to transfer money to cover overdrafts because you didn't check with me first? Or when you bought yourself a VIP seat at the practitioner's conference in the Bahamas, with first-class airfare?"

L. T. grabbed a travel mug from the cabinet.

"Oh, and by the way, you did not bother to see if I wanted to attend. You went to the Caribbean without me for six days. There's a big difference in trying to prevent those scenarios and being controlled."

L. T. pursed his lips tightly but did not respond.

"And talk about controlling behavior, I want my house key back."

L. T. smiled. "All right. I'll get you a key made tomorrow. But this is temporary. You still need to look for someplace else to live. The kids and I want you to move out. We are not changing our minds."

"Why do you have to get a key made? Just give mine back to me." She decided not to touch the demand for her to move out until she spoke with an attorney.

L. T. shrugged. "I had the locks changed."

"Why would you do that?"

"I have my reasons." L. T. poured coffee into his cup.

"And what about Sammy?" Lila pressed. "Where is my dog?"

L. T. pulled his keys from his pocket and stepped into the garage, speaking over his shoulder. "I've got a busy day ahead of me."

Lila rushed forward and grabbed the top corner of the car door to keep L. T. from shutting her out. "Where are you going? And what about Sammy?"

L. T.'s eyes narrowed. "I've got to go. Remove your hands." A wicked smile spread across his face. "I'd hate to accidentally smash them when I close the door. You want a new house key, don't you?"

Feeling defeated, Lila pulled her hands back to her sides. L. T. was still smiling when he backed out of the driveway. No matter how she approached problems with him, Lila could never win. When she arrived at work an hour later, her eyes were red and freshly swollen. As if she hadn't been through enough, Lila was not prepared for what she found when she walked inside.

No one else was there. Lila called Debbie and learned that L. T. had told the staff not to show up to work for her. They complied since they were all afraid of losing their jobs.

Debbie said, "He called and told us you would only come in to treat patients, but all decisions, especially financial and operational ones, would be made by him. But then, he had us cancel all your patients this week."

Lila hurriedly finished the call and called L. T. Of course, he didn't answer.

Lila shook her head. To abate her anxiety, she played solitaire until she won, and deep-cleaned the building. It kept her busy until school let out for Grace. At least she had her baby girl.

Lila arrived at the elementary pickup spot twenty minutes before the bell rang. When Grace saw her car, she sprinted for the rear passenger door.

"Hey, Mommy. I didn't know if you were still coming."

Lila grimaced. "What do you mean?"

"Daddy said you were moving away. I cried because it made me feel sad that you wanted to leave us."

"Oh baby, I'm not leaving you."

"But Daddy said—"

"I don't care what Daddy said!" Lila immediately regretted the strength of her tone and softened it. "I'm sorry. I didn't mean to yell. But I am not moving out of our house."

Grace turned toward Lila. "I told Miss Jacobs I didn't know if I would get to see you again. She let me sit on her lap because I was crying." Grace reached between the seats and snuggled up to Lila. "Are you mad at me, Mommy? I got a good grade on my spelling test. Does that make you happy?"

A tap on Lila's window interrupted the conversation. Grace's teacher.

Lila put down her window.

"I'm sorry to disturb you, Dr. Frost, but Grace made me promise to tell you she did very well on her spelling test today. Ninety-seven percent, one of the highest in the class." The teacher smiled at Grace and leaned in closer to Lila. She whispered, "I'm not sure what's going on with you and your husband, but Grace said he told her she wasn't going to see you again. Just in case, she wanted me to let you know she got a good grade. I think she believes that if she's good enough, you will not leave her."

Lila mouthed, "Thank you for telling me."

The teacher nodded and smiled. "Good luck." She spoke louder and with a cheerful tone. "Bye, Grace. See you tomorrow."

Lila shifted in her seat and wrapped her sweet child in a tight embrace. "Honey, please don't think any of this is happening because of you. You are the best daughter anyone could ask for and I'm so glad you are mine. Daddy and Mommy just need to figure some things out, and we both love you and your brother very much. But even though Daddy and Mommy may not agree about how to plan our lives going forward, we will figure it all out." Lila kissed Grace on the forehead and tousled her hair. "And no matter what anyone else may tell you, I am not going anywhere. You can't get rid of me that easily. You hear?"

Grace frowned. "I don't want to get rid of you, Mommy. But why did Daddy tell me he is kicking you out of your office. He said you are evil, evil, evil. I haven't seen you be bad."

Lila willed the anger rushing up her throat back down. "I don't know why Daddy would say that. You know how kids say things at school that aren't true or nice?"

"Yeah."

"Well, it's like that."

Grace cocked her head and looked at Lila, her bottom lip protruding. "But family should never do that to each other."

"You're right." She couldn't come up with any excuse to cover for L. T. this time, so she deflected. "Tell you what, let's go grab some Chick-fil-A."

"OK." Grace smiled, clapped her hands, and buckled herself into her booster seat.

They arrived home after their snack a little over an hour later. L. T. was gone, but a shiny new house key lay on the kitchen table. At least he'd kept his word about that. However, Sammy was still missing.

Lila was cleaning the kitchen when Debbie called back and confirmed she and the rest of the office staff would return to work the following day. Finally, a little good news.

By 9:30 that night, L. T. still had not returned. Lila tucked the kids in and said prayers with both. Deciding she had as much right to the master bedroom as her husband, Lila showered and climbed into her own bed.

Just before 11:00, the door creaked open. Lila pretended to sleep. She prayed her husband wouldn't hurt her, or worse, try to kill her. Lila didn't put anything past him now, and she regretted not locking herself in.

L. T. shuffled toward the bed. She braced for an attack. Instead, he pulled his pillow from his side of the bed and left. Lila allowed herself to exhale when she heard the shuffle of his feet walking toward the guest room. When he left, she got up and quietly locked the door.

The next morning, L. T. was up before Lila. Matching his initial silence, she moved toward her tea cubby and prepared her wake-up drink.

"You were confrontational last night," he said.

Lila almost dropped the spoon in her hand before spinning around. "Do what?"

"You tried to pick a fight with me."

"I was asleep when you came in." Lila lied. "How can you call that confrontational?"

"I don't think you were really asleep. And you took the bed before I came home. I call that confrontational."

Lila blushed at the truth, even if he was twisting it to claim a false motive. "Can you possibly create any more drama out of thin air? I'm not the one who wants a divorce or who is trying to build a case for one when none exists." Lila lifted her chin and left the room. She hoped she looked more confident than she felt.

L. T.'s car was gone when Lila left for work. She was scheduled to see patients today and felt grateful for the healthy distraction. Everything went smoothly at the office, until mid-morning.

Lila was handing off a patient file when a call came in that Trisha answered. The color drained from her face. She punched the hold button, held the receiver toward Lila, and, though the caller was muted, whispered. "It's your husband, Dr. Frost. He asked to speak with you."

Lila frowned and accepted the receiver. Trisha released the hold. "Hello?"

The chipper timbre of his voice immediately set Lila on edge. "Hey, hon. There's a leak in the basement at the house. The plumber is supposed to come fix it. I told them you'd be home today after 4:00 p.m."

Lila pulled the phone receiver from her ear and looked at it as if it were an alien weapon. Why was L. T. speaking to her as if nothing was happening between them? His up and down mood swings were unsettling. *Why is he acting like he didn't just tell me he wanted a divorce? Like he didn't tell me he wanted me to leave because he and the kids were afraid of me?*

Lila slowly put the receiver back to her ear. "Why are you being so nice to me all of a sudden?"

With an air of innocence, he said, "What do you mean?"

"You know what I'm talking about. You have threatened me. Yelled at me. And tried to convince me I'm the bad guy while you traumatized me the past few days. Don't play stupid, L. T. Frost. Now, what are you up to?"

His laugh sounded more evil than friendly. "I have no idea what you are talking about sometimes. I simply wanted to let you know the repairman was coming. He said he will be there shortly after 4:00."

When he ended the call, Lila knew she had to up her ante in this relational war. She needed proof of what L. T. was doing. Lila realized he was trying to make her look crazy. To what end, she was not certain, but she knew it meant nothing good for her, their children, her dog, or their patients. It was time to start gathering evidence.

Lila asked Debbie to tell the next patient Lila would be a few minutes. Then she went to her office and shut the door.

CHOOSING FORTITUDE

One of the greatest challenges is facing a truth we recognize deep inside but refuse to see and acknowledge with our conscious minds. Healing is impossible if we do not.

Every month, day, and minute we deceive ourselves means one more month, day, and minute we remain in misery. Because when we are not dealing with truth, we are standing on quicksand. Deception of any kind does not offer us the stable ground necessary for mobility and forward movement. Conversely, hard truth gives us a solid path to follow, even when we find it painful to navigate.

If you have a truth gnawing at you, one you desperately try to ignore and hope will go away, try doing the opposite of what your instincts want. Run to reality instead of from it. Rise above the lies—your own emotional ones as well as those others are telling you. Choose fortitude.

The longer you wait, the further freedom will drift beyond your grasp. You may not feel comfortable with or like the facts as they are, but they will never steer you wrong like fear can.

Then you will know the truth,
and the truth will set you free.

—JOHN 8:32

CHAPTER NINE

SHOW ME
the Money

*The real measure of your wealth is how much
you'd be worth if you lost all your money.*

—UNKNOWN

*T*he next day, Lila awoke from another night of little sleep with a banging headache. She didn't drink alcohol, but she imagined this is what others felt when they described their hangovers.

She stumbled toward the shower and, after, fumbled to get her clothes on. Lila didn't bother with makeup and tossed her hair into a ponytail that she twisted into a messy bun.

When she arrived at the practice, Lila entered her security code and headed toward her office, but Debbie met her in the hallway.

"I can't get our computers working today," Debbie said. "None of our scheduling and patient account programs will open. I can't do anything."

"Did you try shutting them down and rebooting?" Debbie looked like she was going to cry.

"I did. Three times. I don't know if the network is down or if it's something else, but the system's been messed up ever since I arrived this morning. We can open our standalone programs, but nothing networked."

Moving into solution mode, Lila said, "Let's see if we can figure this out." She walked toward the back offices with Debbie following close behind.

When Lila opened her office door, she stopped and Debbie bumped into her.

"Oops," Debbie said.

"He took my computer." She gasped and immediately turned toward L. T.'s office. Lila sifted through her keys, unlocked the door, and flung it open. She pointed to L. T.'s empty desk. "His is gone too. You're not going to access any patient accounts. L. T.'s computer also acts as our server."

Debbie moved alongside Lila. "When L. T. said you were having marriage difficulty and told me you were getting a divorce, I never dreamed he would do something like this."

"So, he's been planning this for a while."

"I don't know." Debbie placed a hand on Lila's shoulder.

Lila pushed down overwhelming emotions that threatened to well up. "Let's go back to my office. The hard copies we print every week may not be fully up-to-date but they'll at least help us take care of our patients while I either convince L. T. to bring our computers back or find a way to replace them. Hang with me and help me keep morale up. It looks like we're going old school for a bit."

Back in her own office, Lila opened the petty cash drawer in her desk, lifted out the small box, and unlocked it. It didn't take her long to count the contents. Only $82. "I cannot believe he wiped out petty cash," she said in a half whisper. Lila then logged on to the bank account to check their balance and was dealt another blow.

The balance sat at zero.

"That's not possible!" Lila cried as she picked up the phone to call the bank. She connected with Rebecca at First Federal.

"Hi, Rebecca. This is Lila Frost. I think there is an error in my account balance, and I need you to double check it for me."

"Sure thing, Lila. Give me just a second to pull up your information." Lila heard the clicking of computer keys. "OK, here we go. Oh!"

"What is it?" Lila asked with a sinking feeling in the pit of her stomach.

"This says your account is empty, Lila. Zero."

"That can't be right."

"There's more. Your mortgage payment is scheduled to come out of this account today. Lila, I think you need to come in. It will be easier to review things in person."

More was going on than Lila realized, and she felt torn between fears over her business and her finances. "I'm in the middle of something at the moment," she said. "Can I come in after I straighten this out?"

"Sure. You'll probably want to give yourself at least an hour. I'll let our branch manager know to expect you."

Lila hung up, sighed heavily, and pulled the most recent printed schedule from the corkboard behind her desk. She placed them in the copier and pressed the number two. The machine whirred and spat out the copies. She handed Debbie the copies and kept the originals for herself. "Can you go down to the office supply store and get a whiteboard calendar? We'll use it for scheduling until I get this mess cleaned up. Then create a spreadsheet for documenting records of payments, insurance billing, and other financial details. We'll handwrite notes for patients we see until we can get the computers networked again."

"I'm on it," Debbie said. She placed a hand on Lila's shoulder. "Don't worry, we'll all pull together. You've got support." Debbie left to tackle her mission.

Lila swept a lone tear away from the edge of her eye. She called L. T., but he didn't pick up.

Lila left for the bank with dread hanging all over her. She hoped she could straighten out things quickly and grab the office cash. She needed to buy at least one new computer right away.

Lila walked up to the next available teller at First Federal and asked to speak to the branch manager. "Can you let him know that Dr. Lila Frost is here?"

The young woman phoned the manager. After hanging up, she told Lila that he would be right down and to feel free to have a seat. Lila was too nervous to sit.

Andy Stringer exited the elevator wearing an empathetic expression and a charcoal suit. "Hi, Dr. Frost. Can we go upstairs to my office so we can speak privately?"

"Of course." Lila stepped onto the elevator and tried to hold back the tears as her anxiety fought to take over her entire body.

As they entered Mr. Stringer's office, he gestured for Lila to sit down. "What can I help you with today?"

"Rebecca said there was an issue with my bank account balance."

Mr. Stringer tapped on his keyboard. With a look of concern, he said, "Yes, it appears your account has a zero balance."

Lila could feel the force in her voice. "I'm sorry. I don't understand." She pulled up her business account on her phone. "I should have over $27,000 in that account."

"There was a withdrawal of $30,101.12 yesterday afternoon, just before we closed."

"Who took my money?"

"I understand your frustration, Dr. Frost. Unfortunately, your husband withdrew the money. It's a joint account, Dr. Frost, so you both have equal access to the funds. However, I need to alert you to another activity."

Lila's stomach sunk.

Mr. Stringer glanced at his monitor. "It seems he also withdrew $23,004.87 from your personal checking and $46,419.36 from your personal savings. Both are at zero, and a check was returned on your personal checking this morning. I'm so sorry."

Lila was glad she was already sitting down. "He took almost a hundred thousand dollars? How can he do that without my authorization? Never mind. I know. Joint accounts."

Mr. Stringer paused and continued, "Dr. Frost also accessed your safe deposit box."

"I need to get inside our box right away." Lila's mind reeled. She hadn't been in it for over four years.

"Sure. Follow me and I'll have you sign the card. You just need your key."

"OK," Lila said, following Stringer while fishing for her mostly ignored safe deposit box key. Her heart pounded like the clackety clack of train wheels on a track.

At the vault, Lila signed the card and followed Mr. Stringer inside. He inserted the bank's master key. Lila stepped forward and placed her key into the second lock and twisted the two together in a parallel motion. She swung the small door open and tugged on the handle of the safe deposit box and slid it out easily.

Mr. Stringer led the way to a private viewing room, where he left Lila alone.

Lila gingerly lifted the lid as her heart hammered. She fully expected to find the metal box empty of its contents. Most of it was gone, but she was surprised to discover L. T. had left her something.

Lila pulled out the balled-up piece of paper at the bottom of the box and unwadded the crumpled document. Inside lay L. T.'s wedding ring. Lila palmed it and turned the paper over, wondering what message he may have left. But the page was blank on each side.

Feeling depleted, Lila mustered the energy to close the lid and stepped outside where Mr. Stringer waited. She put the box back into its slot, turned the keys, and pulled hers out. Mr. Stringer removed the master key, and they exited together.

"I hate to bring this up in light of everything you are dealing with, but there is also the matter of the automatic funds transfer for your mortgage. Since the checking account is empty, you'll need to make a payment." Mr. Stringer stopped midway to the lobby and turned toward Lila. "I understand you have a lot to figure out, but after ten days, late charges will be applied. If your loan is thirty days late, it's automatically reported to the credit bureaus. I'm not trying to add pressure, but I don't want you to get blindsided by that either."

"I appreciate your concern," Lila said. "I do have a lot to figure out. I'll let you know something ASAP."

In the main lobby, Mr. Stringer said compassionately, "I wish you the best, Dr. Frost. I hope things work out for you."

Lila's mind searched for answers. How in the world was she supposed to pay the mortgage with no money? Then she remembered the two ATVs in their shed. If L. T. could take all their cash, she could sell their ATVs to make their payment.

Lila immediately called her friend Billie. Only days before, Billie told Lila that she knew someone looking for an ATV. At the time, Lila didn't consider herself a potential seller.

When Billie answered, Lila said, "Is your friend Pete still in the market for an ATV?"

"I can check and get back with you."

Within the hour, Lila was talking to Pete.

"Yeah, I'm interested in both of them," he said. "Could I pick them up next week?"

Lila agreed. It might not resolve her long-term mortgage issue, but for now, she could cover the debt before late charges were incurred.

With the mortgage crisis temporarily handled, Lila focused on her next urgent problem. She headed to Best Buy.

At the store, a friendly young man with sandy hair and eyes that matched the sky-blue polo shirt he wore proved helpful. In twenty minutes flat, he had her set up with a computer system that would provide digital support for the practice in the interim, until Lila could come up with a more permanent resolution for their office.

The clerk placed the computer and its accessories on the counter. "Is there anything else you need?"

"That should do it. Thank you so much." *I'm glad something went right today*, Lila thought.

The young man scanned the boxes. "The total comes to $1,796.17."

Lila tapped her Visa card on the processor.

The clerk's jaw clenched. "I'm sorry, ma'am. It says declined. But try it again, sometimes the reader doesn't work right. Insert the chip this time."

With her taut nerves stretched even tighter, Lila inserted the chip.

After a few seconds, the clerk said, "It's still not going through. Do you have another card?"

"Yes. Give me just a sec." Lila groped for her wallet. When she found it, she slipped her American Express out and showed it to the employee.

"Try that one. Go ahead and insert the chip into the reader."

Lila did, but after a few seconds, the outcome was the same. Her third card, another Visa, did not go through either. She sighed and apologized for taking up his time, and quickly left the store.

In her car, Lila called all three credit card companies. After explaining her situation, the first representative said, "When you opened this account, your husband was made an authorized user versus a joint holder. He can charge, but he is not financially responsible for payments. It says here that you called yesterday to suspend the account."

"I did not suspend my account," Lila said.

"Our records show a call yesterday afternoon from someone claiming to be you who gave us all the right information. We have a recording."

"I will need a copy of that recording," Lila said. "I did not call you yesterday."

Lila called the next two credit card companies. Each representative said the same. But the last conversation revealed even more.

The Amex rep told Lila that L. T. bought three new track phones and spent more than four hundred dollars at Victoria's Secret on that account just two days before removing his name from it.

He obviously planned to leave Lila with the financial responsibility for his fun. And because of fraud originating from somewhere, the cards could not simply be reauthorized for use. Lila would have to complete paperwork and submit proof that she was who she was and that she did not want the accounts suspended.

Just one more stab that L. T. got in.

After trying to reach her husband again, and leaving him yet another voice mail, Lila drove toward the practice. Now livid, she faced the possibility of eking by on paper records and scrounging for funds for an indeterminate future. Not only was Lila crushed by L. T.'s abandonment, but she also had to contend with the chaos he'd created for their practice.

She stopped by the house first. Lila kept a few hundred dollars in her small, personal safe, hidden at the back of her closet. She'd never given L. T. the combination, so at least she could buy food for her and the kids.

Lila hustled up to the front door of her house. She needed to hurry; her employees were waiting for an update, and so were patients.

After unlocking and entering the front door, Lila entered her security code into the alarm system. But instead of the friendly beep and solid green light she was accustomed to, a red light appeared accompanied by a blaring noise. Slow down and concentrate. But a more cautious entry generated the same results. She tried a third time. Again the same obnoxious noise.

Why is my security code not working? I just used it last night.

Knowing that the alarm was going to sound any second, Lila moved on to plan B. She entered Heath's security code and fist-pumped the air when the green light and cheery beep disarmed the system.

Lila made her way to the downstairs spare bedroom. She pilfered through a heavy winter coat and three thick sweaters she kept at the back of the closet purposely to hide her safe. When her fingers wrapped around the metal rectangle, she exclaimed to the empty room, "Gotcha."

A moment later, after turning her key in the safe lock, Lila clutched the cash in her hands, savoring the small sense of safety it represented. She counted out the hundreds, fifties, and twenties carefully. "Five hundred ninety dollars." Then she tucked the money into her wallet, put the safe back where she found it, and climbed the stairs. As she walked down the hallway past her home office, her eyes caught sight of something.

"You've got to be kidding." Lila strode toward her desk. Her very empty desk. The computer, monitor, and even the printer were gone.

Lila ran her hand across the vacant wood surface before screaming, "L. T. Frost, what are you doing to me?" She stumbled to her chair and plopped down, before lifting her eyes to the ceiling. "Lord, let me wake up from this nightmare."

Lila soon got up and made her way to the master bedroom. She needed to give the house a closer inspection. She first went to the closet that held their large safe, the one she and L. T. shared. They kept important papers like birth certificates, passports, and insurance policies in it. The safe also protected her grandfather's coin collection and a moderate amount of cash. With L. T.'s other antics, Lila fully expected the money to be gone.

Lila opened the door on L. T.'s side of the closet. The corner where their safe usually stood like a sentinel was bare. This proved L. T.'s plan to leave her and to strip her of every possible possession.

Lila had no idea how long ago he had taken the safe. Was it when he injured his back? Smudges had disturbed the otherwise perfect square made of dust lines that outlined approximately 150 pounds of protective metal.

Fresh betrayal washed over Lila like a tsunami. She felt a greater urgency to find out what else she didn't know. She called the home security company. A woman named Samantha answered on the second ring.

"I need to check the status of my account," Lila said. "When I arrived home today, my security code wouldn't work."

"I'll be happy to look into this matter for you," Samantha said. "Can I get your first and last name, and a phone number associated with this account?"

"Lila Frost. The account is under L. T. and Lila Frost. Um, excuse me, it's under Leroy and Lila Frost. The phone number connected to the account is mine," Lila said and rattled off the number.

"Thank you, Ms. Frost. Give me just a few minutes to look up your information."

Lila drummed her fingers while she waited. Finally, the representative came back on the line. But her voice sounded unsteady and unsure.

"Well, Mrs. Frost, according to the notes on your account, your husband called yesterday morning. He told us you were going through a divorce, and it was going to get ugly. He asked us to delete your code and change the emergency password and 'everything is OK' password."

"He did what? You can't do that. We are both jointly on the account."

Samantha got her supervisor on the line. After being brought up to speed on the situation, he agreed with Lila and said, "We are going to change everything back to the way it was originally. Nothing will be changed going forward unless we receive written authorization from you both."

"One last thing," Lila said. "Can you please send me an email with everything you have documented on our account from my husband's call yesterday?"

"Of course," the supervisor said. "Since you are a co-owner on the account, you are entitled to the records. I'll copy these notes into an email and send it to you right away."

"Thank you." Lila needed as much evidence as possible to prove what L. T. was doing.

As she was hanging up with the security company, Lila's line beeped with another call. She recognized the bank's number.

"Dr. Frost, this is Mr. Stringer from First Federal."

"Yes."

"A check just tried to clear on your business account. What would you like us to do?"

"I'm afraid you'll just have to send it back," Lila said. "I'll have to deal with any payables that don't clear directly."

"Yes ma'am," Mr. Stringer said. "I'm sorry you are having to go through this."

"Me too."

Grabbing a notebook and pen, Lila moved swiftly from room to room in her house, taking inventory of everything that was missing. When she finished, the list nearly filled a full page. Finally, she felt as if she could go back and face the issues at the practice.

Lila found peace in the afternoon routine of seeing patients. Scheduling proved a bit challenging, but Debbie's spreadsheets allowed for a decently streamlined process. Lila, however, found treating patients without having to deal with insurance paperwork and governmental reports refreshing. Seeing people and not feeling rushed made the workday one of the easiest Lila had ever experienced. It provided a few hours of solace. This tiny positive boost and others like it would help her get through moments that might have otherwise done her in.

SEE TO IT

What would we have if everything we owned disappeared? Most of us will never face such a reality, but if we did, it's good to understand that we can make it. We see many of our fulfilled wants—cell phone, internet, comfy couch—as survival needs, when in fact, we could live without them.

That electricity you enjoy is a convenience. There are other ways to light, heat, and cool. If you lost your internet connection, would it hurt if you did? Perhaps for a few days, or a few weeks, but you would ultimately adapt to life without Wi-Fi more quickly than you realize. After all, we've only had this access for a few years.

TV? Too much is probably doing more harm than good anyway. The car you drive? Instant transportation is a luxury many people around the world don't have. Fast food? A lot of people who say they have no time for cooking would suddenly find some. We might even eat healthier if we had to prepare our own meals and pack our own lunches.

The fact is, sometimes it takes losing something or imagining a loss to comprehend its full value. So, even a loss can become a source of gratitude.

Worrying about possessions or people you might lose—both needed and wanted—won't help. Faith will.

One of the names of God is Jehovah-Jireh, which has been translated to mean "the Lord will provide." You can trust Him. He will not betray or abandon you, and He will see to your provisions. You can count on Him when you can count on nothing or no one else.

There's no greater relief than understanding you are never alone.

*Can all your worries add a single
moment to your life?*

—MATTHEW 6:27 NLT

CHAPTER TEN

LETTING Go

Life moves on and so should we.

—SPENCER JOHNSON

L. T. didn't arrive home until late again, but he must have texted or talked to Heath. After tucking in Grace, and just before her own bedtime, Lila sat on the couch with Heath on the other end. "I wonder where your dad is now and what he's up to?"

"It's none of your business," Heath spat. "You shouldn't be here anyway." He turned back to his phone.

"Who are you texting?" Lila pointed to Heath's hands.

"That is none of your business either."

Lila reached for Heath's cell, but he moved it out of her reach. She tried setting a stern face and speaking with strength. "I am your mother, and it very much *is* my business who you talk to."

Heath did not flinch or falter. "So says you. Dad has a different perspective."

"Is that who you are talking to?"

"Read my lips, Mother." Heath spoke slowly and with emphasis. "It. Is. None. Of. Your. Business!" He stood. "I'm going to bed. I suggest you do the same." His adult tone might have been comical if it wasn't so tragic.

Lila got up to wash some clothes. Physical activity often helped when she felt emotionally off balance. And she had a lot of sadness rolling through her soul. Entering the laundry room did nothing to ease Lila's stress. Piles of towels, underwear, jeans, and shirts of various styles and colors were tossed together. The disarray started in the center hamper marked *BRIGHTS*. The bins on each side, one marked *WHITES* and the other *DARKS*, stood empty. "Why can't my family read and follow directions?"

She bent down and began separating. When that task was complete, Lila started with the largest pile first. "Whites it is," she said to the washing machine. After loading the clothing and adding detergent, she picked up the bottle of chlorine bleach on the shelf just above her head. She shook it. Not even enough for one load.

Lila opened the supply cabinet where she kept extras, and stretched to reach the back left corner. She grabbed the unopened white bottle with blue labeling, pulled, and stopped at a clunking sound.

Curious, Lila strained to get even higher on her toes and felt around with her hand until she touched something small, hard, and square. She wrapped her fingers around the item.

Lila pulled down the object and stared. A cell phone. Obviously a knockoff of the iPhone varieties their family used. Lila turned it over and looked for a brand name. Instead, she discovered a piece of duct tape stretched across the back with *Natalie* written in L. T.'s scrawl with black Sharpie. Lila flipped the phone back to the front and found the power button. When it came on and the pin screen lit up, she instinctively entered L. T.'s commonly used four-number code. The device gave her instant access. "Unbelievable."

She viewed the history. Only one number had ever been called or received. Obviously, the number must belong to Natalie.

Feeling emboldened, Lila grabbed her utility ladder and set it in place in front of the cabinet. She had to know if L. T. was hiding anything else.

Sure enough, in the recesses of the cabinet, Lila found three more phones identical to the first one, except each had a different name on the duct tape. In addition to Natalie, Franny, Chloe, and Kimmy each had their own communication line to Lila's husband. And now she understood how L. T. found her journal. She'd also used the laundry room as a hiding place. He must have run across it when he was scouting a place to stash his own secrets.

Lila climbed down and plopped onto a pile of jeans in a zombie-like fashion. These finds crushed her heart. She needed to take a sad inventory of her married life.

Lila reflected on how many times she had felt so lonely in her marriage that she daydreamed about being in a car accident. She fantasized about her husband realizing how much he loved and wanted her. She imagined him visiting her in the hospital and bringing beautiful flowers. She envisioned his heartfelt apology, saying he couldn't believe he took her for granted before he tenderly kissed her forehead.

But Lila now knew for certain that none of this would ever happen.

She sat on the mound of dirty clothes and finally accepted her harsh reality. Her loneliness was not new. The signs were always there. Her whole relationship with L. T. was a lie. Her husband had faked his feelings for her. He had cheated on her and used her from the moment they met.

And now L. T. was teaching Heath to treat her with the same disrespectful and unloving regard. L. T. hadn't accomplished his goals with Grace yet.

Realizing L. T.'s disrespect now extended to their children, Lila knew she was in danger of losing them permanently. Without them, Lila felt she had nothing left to live for. She could not allow this to happen.

Later that night, while going through the motions of changing into her pajamas, a new wave of desperation washed over her. She got down on her knees beside the bed, folded her hands, and intertwined her fingers before bowing her head onto them.

Lila's voice quivered. "Dear God, I hope you aren't too mad at me." She shifted her body, trying to position her knees more comfortably. "I know you usually don't hear from me except when I ask you for things. I don't blame you if you're frustrated."

Lila paused and waited for God's still small voice. When He didn't speak, she continued.

"Anyway, here I am again. My life is an absolute disaster right now. It seems like everything that's supposed to be right is left and everything left is right. I'm so confused, hurt, and I confess, I'm very angry too."

Again, nothing.

"I try so hard, but nothing is working out for me. What am I missing? Would you tell me what I should do? And please help me not lose my children." Lila opened her eyes, caught herself, and shut them quickly. "I almost forgot, in Jesus' name. And thank you."

Not knowing what else to say, Lila started to move into a standing position. But she stopped herself before standing completely.

She moved her knees back into position. "I'm so sorry, I forgot to ask you to forgive me. I know I've done a lot of things wrong. I put a lot of other things before you—my husband, my children, my practice, my friends, and even Sammy. I'm not grateful like I should be. I apologize for all of it, and for anything I don't remember or don't know I need to be forgiven for. Thank you in advance."

Depleted, Lila stood. As she was folding the comforter and sheet away from her pillows, a thought entered her mind. *Read your Bible.*

"Is that you, God?" Lila said out loud. "Or did that come from my own mind?"

Hearing nothing more, Lila shrugged slightly, opened her nightstand drawer, and pulled out the NIV Bible she kept there.

Lila spoke to the empty room again. "I don't know where I'm supposed to start reading."

After a few minutes of staring at the thick book on her lap, Lila cracked it open near the middle. She allowed the feathery pages to flutter, until they settled in place. "Proverbs 2 it is." She read, starting with verse 1 and speaking every word through 22, the final verse. But she went back and read verses 1 through 11 multiple times. It was as if God was answering her darkest concerns and deepest questions through these ancient passages.

Lila's voice sounded much stronger when she read Proverbs 2:1–11 the fourth time:

My son, if you accept my words
    and store up my commands within you,
turning your ear to wisdom
    and applying your heart to understanding—
indeed, if you call out for insight
    and cry aloud for understanding,
and if you look for it as for silver
    and search for it as for hidden treasure,
then you will understand the fear of the LORD
    and find the knowledge of God.
For the LORD gives wisdom;
    from his mouth come knowledge and understanding.
He holds success in store for the upright,
    he is a shield to those whose walk is blameless,
for he guards the course of the just
    and protects the way of his faithful ones.
Then you will understand what is right and just
    and fair—every good path.
For wisdom will enter your heart,
    and knowledge will be pleasant to your soul.

Discretion will protect you,
and understanding will guard you.

Lila allowed the Bible to rest on her lap while she soaked in the message she'd just read. Peace traveled through her veins as if someone had injected her with a miraculous medicine. She looked toward her ceiling. "Lord, I hear you. I accept your words, I am turning my ear toward your wisdom, and I'm seeking your knowledge and understanding. I trust you to show me what is right and just and fair, every good path. Thank you for protecting and guarding me, and especially my children. In Jesus' name, amen."

Lila laid the Bible carefully back in the drawer, clicked off the light, pulled the covers up to her neck, and rolled over with a satisfied sigh. She felt less alone already. Lila believed she was ready to let her husband go. She was tired of living the insanity of doing the same thing over and over and expecting a different result.

Lila also found a new ability to let her worry go too. She knew she had to give her kids to the Lord, something she never thought she could do. She had to trust Him with the two things that mattered to her most and release them into His protective care. That night, she rested for the first time in weeks.

In the morning, it appeared as if L. T. had not come home at all the night before. The guestroom looked rumpled exactly as it had when L. T. left the bed unmade the previous day. Lila was sure he stayed with Natalie, Franny, Chloe, or Kimmy, but the thought did not sting as much as it would have before.

At breakfast, Heath refused to acknowledge her, though he did eat the pancakes, eggs, and sausage Lila prepared for him.

Grace gobbled hers down. "Thank you, Mommy. That was good."

At least one child was on speaking terms with her.

After the kids left for school, Lila called the practice to cancel all her appointments that day, made another call, showered, and dressed for an appointment with her divorce attorney, Billy Joe Roberts. She gathered the paperwork and cell phones used for L. T.'s mistresses and drove to the attorney's office.

Lila didn't have to wait long in the waiting room, maybe five minutes at most.

"What can I do for you, Mrs. Frost?" said the lean, lanky, fifty-something counselor.

Lila opened her bag and dumped the four phones on his desk. "I found these in my laundry room last night. I'm sure these prove my husband is having affairs with multiple women."

Roberts picked up the one with Franny on the back. "Ah, the old Alcatel 1."

"What is an Alcatel 1?"

"It's a common burner-phone model."

"Burner phone?"

The attorney turned the device over a few times and pressed the power button. "Yeah. A burner phone is a way perps try to keep people from finding out who they are communicating with. Unless you have access to the account information, you cannot trace the calls. They're most often used to cover infidelity or crimes. Do you know the pin code he uses?" Roberts held the phone toward Lila.

Lila took it and punched in L. T.'s pin and handed it back. "I thought I was just being paranoid. Now I realize I should have listened to myself when doubts about my husband crossed my mind."

"I can't say what your husband is doing, precisely," Roberts examined the phone labeled Franny, then picked up the one marked Chloe and extended it for Lila to unlock. "But he's probably up to no good."

A hard shiver reverberated through Lila's body.

Roberts viewed the call log on Chloe's phone and moved on to the device branded for Kimmy. Lila unlocked it, as well. "From first glance, it appears as if he does have a flock of mistresses, and a phone dedicated to each one. I guess he has to write on them so he can keep them straight and not mistakenly call one of his women by the wrong name." Roberts chuckled.

Heat flushed Lila's throat and face.

"Oh sorry, Mrs. Frost. I don't mean to sound so crass and unfeeling. I just see the worst of human nature in my business. You know?"

"I understand," Lila said. "And he has another phone. I found it in his gym bag recently, but it didn't have any tape or name on it. He still has that one."

"Probably a longer-term mistress he's closer to." The attorney thumbed through the call history on Kimmy's phone. He grabbed the last device. Natalie's. After reviewing the call log, he said, "Wow! He talked to this woman over forty hours in one month, excluding their text messages."

Lila's mind wondered at the attorney's comment. How could L. T. spend that much time talking to other women when he barely spoke to her?

"Why don't you tell me everything you know up to this point."

Lila placed a stack of papers on Billy Joe Roberts's desktop. "Where would you like to start? With the money he took out of all our joint bank accounts, the safe deposit box he emptied, or the credit cards he maxed out and canceled? Or would you prefer to discuss how he took computers from our medical practice as well as our home, keeping me from adequate patient care and conducting the admin side of our business? Our dog, Sammy, is missing too. And let's not forget how he is lying and trying to turn our kids against me, all while attempting to convince me I'm crazy. Who knows? He may be plotting to kill me, too, for all I know."

Roberts put up both hands to stop her. "OK, OK. I get it. Let's take one thing at a time. Has there been any abuse?"

Lila pondered before speaking. "Not physical, no. However, my mom has always told me that L. T. mentally and emotionally abuses me. She says he's arrogant and cocky and always has to be the smartest person in the room, no matter who he's talking to. And I cannot argue with her. No one is going to tell L. T. how to do anything."

"Can you provide specific examples of what that looks like?" Roberts poised a pen over a legal notepad.

Lila spewed years' worth of painful stories over the next three hours while her attorney scribbled notes in his homespun style of shorthand. She left at lunchtime. Although depleted, Lila felt relieved to have started the process. Grateful she wasn't scheduled to see patients, she needed time to rest her mind and body before she began tackling the tasks her lawyer assigned her. The first of which was to apply for a new credit card. Her credit wasn't yet ruined, so getting a new card would be easy enough.

After starting the car, Lila looked in the mirror and repeated her affirmations. "I deserve to be loved. I am valuable. God loves, values, and cherishes me. I am going to love, value, and cherish me today."

A little part of her started to believe it.

COMING TO TERMS

Often, we know what we should do, but we question our insights and wisdom. Sometimes, the voice of God is shouting in our spirit, but we douse his voice with our human insecurity and doubts. We wrestle with indecisiveness only because we refuse to believe the information literally in front of our eyes, ears, and minds.

Letting go doesn't mean denying the truth. Letting go means releasing emotional lies that keep us imprisoned and prevent us from acting on facts necessary for our health and the soundness of others. Letting go is taking your honest concerns and burdens to Christ and laying them at His feet, where you invite Him in and ask Him to guide and help you figure things out. Letting go is starting the forgiveness process for ourselves as well as for others.

When we give ourselves permission to face our fears, we are released to begin our healing and restoration journey. We become free to live in a more balanced and full way.

When we accept the help of Jesus, acknowledge His power, and allow Him to lift the weight, we rise to that space where our spirits can truly soar.

Come to me, all you who are weary and burdened, and I will give you rest. Take my yoke upon you and learn from me, for I am gentle and humble in heart, and you will find rest for your souls. For my yoke is easy and my burden is light.

—MATTHEW 11:28–30

CHAPTER ELEVEN

MEANINGS AND
Mental Resilience

If your heart is broken,
make art with the pieces.

—SHANE KOYCZAN

*L*ila awoke from a much-needed nap in time to start dinner. She decided on homemade Salisbury steaks with brown gravy, roasted green beans, baked potatoes, and a fresh, green salad. She even whipped up a strawberry shortcake for dessert. The house smelled amazing, lifting Lila's mood. Until Heath strolled in after school.

"What are you still doing here?"

The interrogatory tone did not escape Lila's notice. She decided not to play into the drama and pretended her son didn't wish she were gone. Lila added an enthusiastic tone to her voice. "I'm making supper. Everything from scratch."

Heath picked up the packet of brown gravy mix and smirked. "Really?"

Lila remembered Billy Joe Roberts's admonishment. "Don't let L. T. or Heath rattle you. Act normal, like the good wife and mama you are."

Lila forced a smile. "Well, almost everything is homemade. I'm making Salisbury steaks and all the fixings. Dinner should be ready by 6:00."

"I'm not eating it. Dad and I are doing something else tonight. Grace is going with us too."

"Where are you going?"

"If you must know, we are going to look at houses. Since you are making things hard on Dad, he's going to take the high road and be the one to move out. And we're going with him."

Lila stepped toward her son, hoping to hug him.

Heath pulled back, his face painted with a look of horror. "Don't you touch me. I'll call 911."

Lila gasped. "Why would you say such a thing? You know I'm not going to hit you."

"I *don't* know that." Heath took a step back.

Lila held her arms open in a welcoming invitation. "I'm your mom. I would not hurt you for the whole world. You mean everything to me. Please believe me."

"You scare me."

"But I've never given you reason to feel afraid of me," Lila said. "Why are you suddenly scared of me now?"

Heath grunted. "We're going with Dad tonight. I'm not arguing with you anymore."

"But Heath—"

"I said I'm not arguing. I'm moving out with Dad, and I'm not eating your crappy food." Heath dismissed Lila like an irritating gnat with a wave of his hand and left the room.

Lila slumped into a chair. How was she going to maintain her energy for a battle not only with her husband but also with her son?

Lila's cell chirped. She sniffed before answering.

"Hey, my friend."

Tiffany. Lila wished she hadn't answered, even though she hadn't talked with her friend in a few weeks.

"What are you up to?"

"Nothing." Lila didn't feel like talking to anyone in her current state of mind. "I fixed a beautiful dinner, but L. T. is taking the kids house hunting tonight. I guess I'm on my own." She hated the deep melancholy she heard in her own voice.

"Good. Well, I don't mean good that you are going through this, but good that we can spend time together. Why don't we go grab a bite?"

"I don't know. I'm not really in the mood to go anywhere or to see people."

"That's precisely why we need to get you out. Wallowing in misery never helped a single person feel better. You have to force yourself to do things when you're depressed. After enough time, the feelings will follow. But you may need to push yourself for a while. I know, I've been there."

Lila did not like feeling pressured. "I hear what you're saying, and I know you mean well, but I seriously don't want to leave my house."

"And that's why I'm not taking no for an answer. You can eat what you cooked tomorrow. I'll be there in half an hour to take you out for dinner." Tiffany hung up before Lila could protest further.

When they walked into Dominic's Italian restaurant, Lila regretted caving to her friend's invitation. It felt like every set of eyes was boring into her. Did these people know her husband and children believed life would be better without her?

The maître d' escorted the two women to a small table tucked into an intimate corner near the upscale bar. After ordering calamari and lemon waters, they discussed the entrée options and Lila's predicament.

"I think I'm going with the caprese chicken," Tiffany said. "I'm famished."

Lila smiled. "That sounds good, but I think I'll just have the Italian wedding soup. I don't think my stomach can handle anything too heavy right now."

"It's crazy how our emotions affect our appetite." Tiffany snapped her napkin and placed it in her lap and eyed the calamari the server placed in the middle of the table.

After taking their orders, the server said, "Will there be anything else?"

"No, thank you," said Lila.

Flexing a muscled arm, Tiffany picked up a crispy appetizer strand. "I love these things."

Lila wished she were in half as good a shape as her triathlete friend. She grabbed some strips for herself.

"How are you holding up?" Tiffany said.

Lila played with her food. "I guess all right. The more I'm finding out about L. T., the more I realize I don't know him and likely never have. My attorney suggested I hire a private investigator. But that seems over the top to me."

"You should probably listen to him." Tiffany sipped her water.

"Maybe you're right," Lila said. "Something has to change. He's turned Heath against me. He's trying to turn Grace. He's taken all our money, removed most of the computers at home and the practice, and even undermined my access to our home security system and credit cards. And Sammy's missing too." She hung her head. "I feel like the most naive person in the world. I just want my life to go back to the way it was."

Tiffany patted Lila on the hand. "I'm going to challenge your thinking. But all in the spirit of care and concern. Is that OK?"

"Do I have a choice?"

Tiffany laughed. "Not really. But I promise, I want nothing more than to speak the truth in love."

"I'm used to people telling me I'm wrong anyway. I've lived with it my whole life. So, challenge away."

Tiffany squeezed Lila's hand tenderly. "I want you to really hear yourself. Listen to your own thoughts and analyze them. What are you telling yourself?" Tiffany squeezed Lila's hand again. "For instance, you just told me you wanted your life to go back to the way it was."

"And?"

"And is that true? We may not see each other as often as we would like, but I've been around you enough through the years to notice how L. T. talks down to you and demeans you. He may not physically abuse you, but the mental, emotional, and verbal abuse you are subjected to is blatant." Tiffany leaned forward. "For pity's sake, we couldn't even have dinner like this before he announced he wanted a divorce. And yet, I'd wager that if he wasn't initiating this separation, you would still be living under his thumb. If he wanted to use you for his pleasure, he did. Otherwise, he tossed you in the corner like his personal rag doll."

Lila cringed at her friend's hurtful insights. Weakly, she said, "But I love him."

"OK, I'm going to throw another challenge your way. Do you love yourself?"

Lila paused before saying anything. When she did speak, she stammered. "I. Well, I. Um, I'm working on it."

"I believe it's high time you did," Tiffany said. "You are fearfully and wonderfully made, and that is a beautiful thing. Our very conception and creation give us reason to celebrate."

Lila noticed the similarity in this line of thinking with the affirmations Billie had taught her to use. She had to admit that shifting to this type of intentional focus did help.

The waiter brought their food and the women scooted back to make room for it. When the server left the table, Tiffany resumed the conversation.

"It's time for you to stop letting others undervalue you. Value yourself."

There was that word *value* again. Lila's eyes glistened. She took a bite of soup to mask the emotions threatening to take over her body.

Tiffany softened her tone. "I hope you know I'm only saying these things because I care about you so much. You are my friend and I do love you. I cannot possibly describe how difficult it's been to watch a smart, capable, beautiful, compassionate, kind, and wonderful woman allow herself to be cheated on and belittled."

Lila sighed. "When I hear you describe everything you just said, it makes perfect sense. And I know it's the type of thing I would say to another woman in a position like mine. But I do not understand myself. I have a doctorate and I run a thriving medical practice. I know I'm capable and strong when it comes to our business. So, why do I let my husband wipe his feet on me? Why have I done that all these years? And now my son is starting to treat me like his dad does." Lila picked up another piece of calamari and toyed with it. "How can I be one way at work but entirely different at home with my family. Am I just an impostor?"

"I don't think you're an impostor," Tiffany said. "I think you simply have some areas in your life where you are allowed to live like your authentic self and others where you have become so conditioned by threats that you no longer let yourself try there. You've been shut down, and now you shut yourself down before others get the opportunity to do it to you. But remember, just because it is or has been does not mean it has to continue that way. You have a choice and can start making changes. Now. In this moment and beyond."

Lila sighed again. "I wouldn't even know where to start."

Tiffany leaned forward. "Find something to hold on to. A symbol that represents your resolve."

"Like what?"

Tiffany paused for a moment. "Is there something that represents positive energy for you?"

"There is a flower I really like," Lila said. "It stands for strength and inspiration."

"Tell me about it. What specifically do you like?"

"It's the alstroemeria."

"Alstrowhat?" Tiffany laughed.

Lila smiled. "It's pronounced, al-strow-meh-ree-uh."

Tiffany opened her phone and googled while the server refilled their waters. "Aha, here it is," she said and looked up. "It's pretty."

Lila nodded when Tiffany showed her the phone screen. "It is beautiful. But it's what it stands for that draws me to it. The alstroemeria symbolizes friendship and devotion, and the twists in the flower symbolize the trials and tribulations of friendships. I think a lot of women are like alstroemeria. They start out a little reserved and simple, like small buds, but then they blossom into gorgeous flowers, getting stronger with maturity. The alstroemeria are resilient, their blooms last a long time—like women. I keep waiting to grow into my alstroemeria season."

"That's really beautiful," Tiffany said. "And you are beautiful, just like the alstroemeria. You are blossoming like the alstroemeria. And you are resilient like the alstroemeria. This is your season."

"I like that." Lila did a quick google search of her own. She screenshotted a particularly vibrant photo of an alstroemeria, and made it her lock screen. "My new inspiration," Lila held the phone up for Tiffany to view.

"I love it." Tiffany smiled. "Now you can look at that encouragement anytime something or someone starts to bring you down."

"I will do that. Thank you so much."

"My pleasure."

Lila put her phone down. "I'm glad you got me out of the house tonight. I'm also grateful you've never given up on me. Friends like you are rare." Lila picked up a spoonful of soup. "And suddenly, I'm famished too. Of course, unlike you, I could stand to drop a few more pounds, even though all this stress has helped me lose some weight."

"Oh, my friend. I see nothing but excellence when I look at you. Stop being so hard on yourself and start choosing to love you for who you were created to be." Tiffany patted Lila's hand.

"Even though I thought I'd overcome it, I guess I still struggle with old messages that made me feel fat when it wasn't true. I need to work on that too."

Tiffany leaned back in her chair. "If you want to work on your health, we can talk about that, but another time, OK? Right now, I want you to simply focus on appreciating you, exactly as you are, made in God's perfect image. Now let's enjoy our meal and this awesome chance to spend time together."

"Yes, ma'am." Lila smiled and dipped her spoon into her soup.

For the rest of the evening, the two women gabbed, laughed, and focused on nothing more than good food and a great friendship. At the evening's end, Tiffany dropped Lila at home. They hugged goodnight before Lila got out of the car. As she was walking to her front door, Tiffany called, "Hey."

Lila swung around.

"Don't forget to smell the alstroemerias." Tiffany grinned and waved before backing out of the driveway.

Lila smiled, determined to follow her friend's advice. That evening had given her much to think about. Lila resolved to make several additional changes.

Maybe, she *was* entering a new season.

OPEN YOUR HEART

When we feel betrayed, battered, and broken, our first instinct is to hermit in a safe place—alone. We can become so self-protective that we fear letting anyone else in. This is especially true when we are wounded by someone we trusted, someone we allowed into our intimate spaces.

But we must guard against projecting our feelings onto everyone else we meet or interact with. Just because one or some behaved hurtfully does not mean everyone is like them.

If we realize we are stuck in a pattern of attracting people who cause us pain, the time is likely right to seek professional insight and guidance. A safe person in ministry or a certified therapist, facilitated group sessions or coaching—all of these are options for finding someone experienced and/or qualified to help you identify issues and overcome unhealthy habits.

Be warned. Not everyone who has credentials will either be the right fit for you or have motives that align with your needs. Some may not have the knowledge for your circumstances.

Even though you've decided to open your heart, you must still exercise wisdom. If you sense that something isn't right with the person or group you are seeing, do not hesitate to find a better alternative.

Seek the balance between healthy self-respect and boundaries and looking for and finding the best in other people.

The LORD is close to the brokenhearted
and saves those who are crushed in spirit.

—PSALM 34:18

CHAPTER TWELVE

CLEANING
House

Emptiness has its solace in that there's nothing left to take.

—ANI DIFRANCO

*L*ila hung up her phone and stared at the number she'd scratched on the notepad in front of her. Billy Joe Roberts sounded pleased when she'd asked for the name and contact information for the private investigator that he referred. Lila hoped she was making the right decision.

When she read the note she'd found from Heath first thing that morning, Lila renewed her decision to be proactive. She lifted the ripped piece of paper off the counter and read Heath's scrawl again. "We're with Dad for the day. Don't wait around."

Lila dialed Marc Bansmith, Private Investigator.

He picked up on the second ring and greeted the caller.

Lila almost ended the call before she said a word. But she reflected on the conversation with Tiffany the previous night and reminded herself to remain resilient like the alstroemeria.

The PI repeated himself. "Hello?"

"Yes. Uh. Hi. My name is Lila Frost."

Bansmith sounded irritated. "What can I do for you, Ms. Frost?"

"My attorney, Mr. Roberts, said I should hire you."

"Who did you say your attorney was?"

"Billy Joe Roberts."

"Oh, gotcha. I know two attorneys with the last name Roberts. Go ahead."

"My husband has asked for a divorce." Once the first words tumbled out of Lila's mouth, they cascaded like a waterfall. "I don't want it, but he isn't giving me a choice. One minute I feel strong, like I'm better off without him. I'm beginning to realize he's never really treated me like he loved me. And I found out he's been cheating on me. Maybe for years. I'm not really sure. That's one of the things I need you to find out."

The investigator made a noise, but Lila continued undeterred. "Even though he acts like he wants me dead, I still love him. That's why I cry my eyes out one minute, wishing he would come back, but then feel like I'm ready to move on the next. Our finances and business are a whole other disaster, he—"

"OK," Bansmith spoke with an even, matter-of-fact tone. "Let's back up and slow down. I understand you are emotional, Mrs. Frost."

"I'm sorry."

"No need to apologize, emotions are real and understandable in these kinds of situations. But I work with verifiable evidence only. So, I will always pull us back to the facts."

Lila felt a bit scolded. "Sure."

"Now, when can you come into my office? I'll need any documentation you have, including photos, as well as known schedules and routines of your husband."

"Do you have any openings tomorrow morning?"

"Can you make it early? Say, 7:30?"

"Yes. I can do that."

Bansmith rattled off his address and ended the call.

Now Lila was thankful she had listened to her attorney and applied for a new credit card. She went to get a new laptop and printer.

After returning home with her purchases and setting them up, Lila spent the better part of two hours printing account records, email threads, other documents she'd found and saved, and some photos from the internet and her computer. She also dug through boxes and drawers to find handwritten notes, cards, and a few doodles and drawings L. T. had done that seemed like they might be pertinent. She made copies of everything, and when she finished, had to cram the lid on a banker's box.

Stepping back, Lila realized those papers represented years of denial on her part. She'd lied to herself a long time about the kind of person she'd married. A rumbling noise disrupted her thoughts.

Following the sound, Lila strode to her front door. She opened it and stepped onto her front porch, blinked twice, and stared at the white-and-green moving truck backing into her driveway.

L. T. paced in the street and moved his arms like an airplane traffic director. The big rig squealed to a stop just in front of the garage doors.

Lila ignored her agitated husband and marched toward the driver and passengers spilling out of the cab. "Excuse me, can I help you?"

One of the men looked at the clipboard in his hand. "Is this Dr. L. T. Frost's residence?"

"Yes. I'm Dr. Lila Frost. What can I do for you?"

The man waved the clipboard toward Lila. "Says here, we're supposed to move the furniture from this address to 1492 Sycamore Lane."

"Not all of it," Lila said. "There must be some mistake." She glared toward L. T.

"I have Dr. Frost's signature right here." The man offered the clipboard to Lila for review. "It says to move all furnishings. There's nothing about leaving anything behind."

L. T. had clearly signed his name.

"Please hold on," Lila said. "Don't do anything yet. I'll see if I can get this cleared up."

"Sure thing, ma'am. But we can't wait too long. We need to get started soon. We still have to unload at the other location."

"I'll be right back." Lila made her way toward her husband.

L. T. ended a phone conversation when Lila approached. "Don't start." He put his hands up as if to defend himself. "I have the police on notice."

She turned back toward the movers. "He's only lying if his lips are moving," she shouted. Lila couldn't believe she spoke up like that.

Then she directed her attention back to L. T. and let an accumulation of frustration pour out. "Don't start? Not only do you betray my trust over and over again, walk out on me, try to take the kids from me, ruin me financially, but you think you're going to take my furniture too?" Lila parked her hands on her hips but kept her tone level though determined. "Your abuse stops here right now. I don't want to fight with you, but I'm not going to lie down and let you walk on me anymore. I have no problem with you taking what belongs to you, but you are not taking anything of mine."

L. T. stared at her. For once, he did not open his mouth to respond.

Lila wheeled around and walked back to the moving crew, targeting the man with the clipboard. "OK. You are not to touch anything of mine. I will approve every item you load. If I say no, it stays. Are we clear?"

"As long as the guy who signed off on the order agrees, I'm good with it. Makes no difference to me," he said and looked toward L. T. "You good with this?"

"Yes, I guess." L. T. waved a hand in the air and turned away.

Lila followed the moving crew inside and went room by room with them, using tape to mark furnishings they could remove. When she stepped outside and stood by the door for added oversight, Lila noticed L. T.'s car was gone. She couldn't believe he'd given up.

Hours later, the man in charge asked Lila to inspect the contents of the truck.

"I watched you take everything out, so I'm satisfied."

"Oh no, I'm not taking a fall," he said. "I need you to inspect the truck and sign off."

Lila shrugged and walked behind the truck where a worker waited to close the doors to the trailer. One item caught her eye. She had initially approved its removal. She stepped forward, reached inside, and grabbed an object casually thrown on top of a box near the back.

When the truck lurched onto the street, Lila clutched the alarm clock in her hands. For her, it symbolized freedom. L. T. would no longer dictate when she woke up, or anything else for that matter. Lila may not have wanted this divorce, but even in her state of sadness and anger, she felt a spark of hope.

For the first time ever, this was her chance to start living on her own terms.

Lila committed to letting L. T. make his own mistakes without her interference or disruption. She realized if she tried to control too much, the truth might not reveal itself. She had to trust that her husband's real colors would eventually show and allow legal decision-makers to see what was best for her children.

FEARING LONELINESS

One of the great fears common to women and men throughout the ages is isolation. We struggle, fight, and avoid anything that might force us into the great emptiness of feeling alone.

And yet, it is often in solitude where we find our true selves, where we dare to explore our deepest thoughts, feelings, and desires, discovering our actual needs and how to fulfill them.

Sometimes we are thrust, kicking and screaming, into the abyss of a solitary season. But in that desert of desolation, we are like seeds planted in dark soil. Our roots dig deeper. The fertilizer of events feeds us wisdom. Our tears, like water, soften our souls and crack our hard shells allowing compassion and empathy for others to sprout. We are comforted in our sufferings, so we in turn learn to comfort others in their sorrows.

And in the darkness, God works. We are never truly alone—no matter what our emotions tell us.

When terrible, uncontrollable, blindsiding situations strike, we commonly question, *Why, God, are you allowing this to happen to me?*

But even if we don't know all the details of what's occurring beneath the surface of our situation, we can take our questions to God. When we let Him lead us versus being driven by desperation, we can trust, even when we don't see His hands at work. If we open our minds and spirits to hear Him in our sad states, if we stop fearing loneliness, He will begin to show us opportunities.

Only God can see into the future, where our greatest heights are attained. He knows our potential when we feel like we've failed at everything. It's when we hold on to hope in the abyss that we find our real roots sprout there.

Now faith is confidence in what we hope for
and assurance about what we do not see.

—HEBREWS 11:1

CHAPTER THIRTEEN

REVELATIONS

*I will not let anyone walk through my mind
with their dirty feet.*

—GANDHI

L. T. didn't just move his things out of the house, he took their children with him. Of course, he brought Grace back within forty-eight hours when he realized how much effort it took to care for a six-year-old.

Grace wasn't as self-sufficient or pliable as Heath. She questioned pretty much everything and retained a lot of loyalty to her mother, especially when it came to "Daddy's new girlfriend."

Five weeks after the moving-truck incident, Lila had her second appointment with Marc Bansmith, PI. She'd brought him data and details last time, now it was his turn to deliver information gathered from his investigation.

Bansmith grinned at Lila after seating her in the chair across from his desk. "I think you're going to be pleased with all the dirt I've unearthed on your husband," he said. "L. T.'s been a busy boy." The investigator patted four manila folders, each at least two inches high.

Pleasure wasn't what Lila felt. "I'm ready." She stiffened her spine.

"I know we've reviewed a lot of financial data over the past few weeks on our phone calls," Bansmith said. He slid the top folder off the stack and laid it aside. "I was able to verify some additional porn site charges on a credit card you weren't aware he was using. We're up to just under $52,000 in money he's spent on his sexual proclivities."

"Great," Lila said. "I'm starting to think nothing my husband does will surprise me anymore."

Bansmith put a hand on the stack of folders. "I've also discovered some other charges, and I'll tell you about those in a few minutes. But let's start with the issue that's going to offer you the best strategy for winning in court. His women. The other financial matters tie to this anyway."

Lila stifled a moan. "Having evidence about his affairs may help me win in court, but regardless, L. T.'s adultery makes my kids and me losers." Even though she was beginning to adapt to life on her own, it still stung Lila to think about her husband sleeping around.

"Don't let your pain take your focus off what you need to do. Remember what I told you, the one with the best documentation typically ends up the winner. And you said you need to be that person for your children, especially your little girl."

"I do." Lila nodded.

Bansmith pulled the thickest folder from the pile and shoved the others to his left. He flipped it open and pulled out a few pages stapled together. "I was able to trace L. T. to an online profile on a couple of dating sites. His username and bio are the same on each. I'll let you read them for yourself. I included them in my summary report." The PI extended the stapled pages to Lila.

After skimming the introductory sections of Bansmith's summation, Lila read in earnest at the third paragraph.

The username, DrHouseCall, refers to Dr. Leroy Travis Frost, a/k/a L. T. Frost, husband of Lila Frost, client. His bio reads: For the right woman, this doctor definitely makes house calls. I'm hot and ready in the Scarborough area. Will drive up to 100 miles each way to meet a lady of my liking. My hobbies include working out, golf, and romantic dinners in exotic locales. I enjoy steamy beverages and steamier conversations.

Lila snorted. "Romantic dinners in exotic locales? Who's he kidding? His idea of romance is asking what's for dinner and when it will be ready. And he won't touch a hot drink of any kind."

Bansmith chuckled but quickly turned serious. "Unfortunately, it appears he's had some takers. I even found an online mapping tool he uses for planning and marking where each woman is located and their hookup spots. Apparently, he enjoys the strategy as much as the execution."

"Sounds like L. T.," Lila said. "OK, what else do I need to know?"

"After interviewing some of your neighbors, employees, and anyone else who may have had recent contact with your husband, I think we've got at least six or seven willing to sign affidavits and testify. Most of them said he had made sexualized comments toward or about them or other women."

Lila crossed her hands in her lap.

"He even went so far as to flirt with the female officer who arrested him on the child predator allegations. She said after he calmed down in the squad car, he told her she had the most beautiful eyes he'd ever seen. On the drive to the precinct, he told her she filled out her uniform to perfection. She said he used a sultry voice, and it was so sickening that she's never forgotten the encounter."

Goosebumps prickled Lila's skin. "Why would he act like that?"

"I see all manner of bad behavior in my field of work. Who knows why some people do what they do? But frequently, wives like you are blindsided by a man who wears different personas, depending on who he is with. In your husband's case, I can tell you it's been going on for a while. Three of your neighbors stated they have witnessed him bringing women in and out of your house on days you were working."

"What?" Lila wanted to vomit. "He brought women into our home? Where we lived with our children?"

"I'm sorry I had to be the one to tell you this."

Lila stood. "Excuse me." She ran out the door and hoped she could get to the bathroom in time.

Once her gag reflex turned to dry heaves, Lila collapsed on the ladies' room floor. Over the last few weeks, she had processed and come to terms with L. T.'s infidelity. But finding out he had engaged in sex with other women, plural, in "their" home caused a visceral reaction. Lila turned her attention away from the toilet and drew her knees to her chest, rested her elbows on top of them, and dropped her forehead onto her hands.

Lila focused her thoughts, willing the disturbing images of her husband and other women out of her head. Appreciate the alstroemeria. Stand strong. You did not ask for this, and your husband's poor choices are not your fault. Don't let his actions strip you of your resilience. God loves you and He is with you.

After successfully capturing her pain-filled thoughts and replacing them with affirming ones, Lila stood. She straightened her shoulders and walked back to the private investigator's office. She tapped on the doorframe and poked her head in. "Mr. Bansmith?"

"Are you all right?"

"I am now. I apologize. I just wasn't mentally prepared to find out he brought those other women into my home."

"Understood. Do you think you can handle the rest of what I have to tell you?"

Lila sat again and took a long breath. "I'm ready. I can do this," she said, more for her own benefit than for his.

Bansmith pointed to another page. "I've also documented your husband's purchases for several sex enhancement apparatuses. You will need to examine the dates he bought them to see if they align with your," he cleared his throat before continuing, "your sexual activity with your husband. I am working on matching them up with the information I found on his meet-up mapping and planning tool."

"I won't be able to help with that," Lila said. "One of the things I'm struggling with is how active our sex life was until the day he left. I don't understand his ability to carry on with so many women while continuing to have sex with me. We were, uh, *very* active." A burning sensation blushed her face.

"You'd be surprised at how many men pull that off," Bansmith said.

Lila swallowed. Her mind resurrected memories of condoms she'd found in her husband's bathroom vanity even though he had a vasectomy after Grace was born. In recent weeks, Lila also discovered other sexual paraphernalia he used for his pleasure, not for hers. Again, she wondered how she'd missed so much.

Bansmith sifted through pages until he found the document he searched for and continued. "When I got into your husband's cloud account—"

"So the possible passwords I gave you worked?"

"Like a charm. I found pictures, including selfies your husband took of himself with various mistresses." The PI slid copies in front of Lila.

Lila glanced at the one on top. Color drained from her face. "This was taken in my office," she said pointing to L. T. and one of his lovers.

"Unfortunately, I don't think he has very discriminating taste about where and with whom he, uh, gets intimate."

"No kidding."

"Your husband also has a favorite florist he likes to use for sending bouquets to his girlfriends." Bansmith pulled out a file folder he titled Flowers by L. T.

"A florist?" Lila said in disbelief. "He's never bought me flowers. I begged him to do something like that for me, but he always refused. Even when we were dating."

"I have copies of several invoices. He spent an average of $100 per arrangement. And they almost always included a love note, especially to his five favorites."

"Love notes? L. T. doesn't do love notes." Lila slumped in her chair.

Bansmith lifted the sheet of paper in his hands. "Each one is usually a similar form of the same message. 'I love you. I'm sorry I couldn't be with you last night. I missed you and can't wait to see you.'"

"And who are these five favorite women you mentioned?"

"The same ones you found the burner phones for, except for one."

"And who is she?"

"The woman he's living with now. I assume he had a burner phone for her as well, probably the one you found in his gym bag. Her name is Raven. She's a stripper in Wideview."

Lila gulped. "L. T. is living with a stripper? And my son is living in the same house with them?"

"Yes, and yes," the investigator said. "I also verified he's still seeing at least three of the women, including Chloe. I spoke to her. If it's any consolation, she's a nice girl. A whore. But a nice girl."

Lila shook her head at the irony of his statement. "That is no consolation at all, Mr. Bansmith," she said. "It does not change the fact that he was sleeping with me while having sex with countless women. And each one of them probably had other sexual partners, as well. Plus, my son is living with someone who works in the sex trade."

"Of course. I apologize if I insulted you by using the word *whore*."

"That is not my issue," Lila said. "But, maybe it should be."

"Of course," Bansmith said. "Sorry for that. All right, let's get back to business." He riffled past several documents and pulled out another paper-clipped set. "So, that about takes care of my internet findings. Oh wait, I did forget one thing. Your husband started renting a post office box about—"

Bansmith went back to the page he'd had in his hand before. He ran his finger down the document. "Here it is. He started renting a post office box about four years ago. This is where he had his shipments from sex shops sent to. Most of those purchases were for sex enhancements and toys, and he bought them using an American Express ending in 2491. This is his secret card. All the subscription fees for his pornography sites were paid by this card too. I figure he spent about $16K alone over the past year."

Lila blew out a long breath. She really didn't know the man whom she shared the marital bed with.

"According to the paper trail I've followed, the Amex bill was automatically deducted out of a checking account he had in his name alone. The transfer on death was assigned to your son, Heath. But the deposits made in that account look like they came from checks drawn as distributions on your clinic's account."

Lila rolled her eyes. "I am continually stunned to find out what a fool I was. He did all this under my nose. I did not know about his secret mailbox, credit card, or checking account."

"Don't beat yourself up too much. Thousands of highly intelligent and successful women are duped every day by men with nefarious motives and tactics. And there are plenty of women who are equally as guilty of taking men to the cleaners and worse. I see it all. But as much as I could become completely jaded, I make sure I look for positives in people."

Lila murmured to herself. "I need to be strong for the kids. I need to focus on the pure, good, admirable, excellent, and lovely."

"I didn't catch that last part," Bansmith said.

"It's just a Bible scripture. Philippians 4:8."

"Good one."

Lila smiled weakly.

The investigator continued his report with an offhanded remark. "I assume you're aware your husband took out a million-dollar life insurance policy on you last year, making himself the beneficiary."

"We both have million-dollar policies. But we took those out right before we got married. I just changed my beneficiary from L. T. to my mom," Lila said.

"Yes, I have record of those. But this is an additional million-dollar policy. Like I said, he just took it out last year. Did you know about it?"

"No," Lila said. "I did not. But I've had this sick, worried feeling. Do you think he's trying to kill me or drive me to suicide?"

Bansmith lifted up his hands. "Let's not make assumptions. Remember, in addition to my other methods, I had you go to the DMV to verify his vehicle was in both of your names, which allowed me to put a GPS tracker on it. And to date, I've seen nothing alarming in his messaging or movements. Unless you count his sexual escapades and what he's done with your money, that is. But I'll keep watching."

Lila did not feel comforted. She knew L. T. was a coward but her husband had told her more than once, "You don't exist. No one will notice you are gone."

"I do have some good news." Bansmith smiled.

"Hallelujah," Lila said.

"I found your dog."

"You know where Sammy is?" Lila scooted to the edge of her chair.

"Yes, your husband gave him to a couple over in Springfield. I've got their contact info in my summary report, so you can arrange to get him back." Bansmith pointed to the document he'd handed Lila earlier.

Lila's heart swelled.

"That about wraps up all I've got so far. I think there's probably enough for court, but see what your attorney says. I will forward digital copies of what I have in my files to both you and your attorney." He patted the manila folders he had begun to restack. "And I will keep an eye out for anything that might signal danger for you. I promise."

"I appreciate that," Lila said. "And thank you for this." She waved the summary report in the air. "At least I can try to get my Sammy back."

Ten minutes later, Lila stepped into the sunlight and squinted. She looked around cautiously and slipped her sunglasses over her eyes. Ever since she discovered her husband was a pathological liar, she didn't trust any place or person.

Lila breathed easier when she made it inside her car and hit the button to lock all her doors. Having taken the whole day off, she drove home. Lila had also arranged for Grace to go to a friend's house after school to spend the night. Lila hadn't known exactly what Marc Bansmith would reveal before she met with him, but she had the foresight to recognize her need to deal with some pretty strong emotions afterward. And now she knew exactly what to do.

At home, armed with her cleaning caddy, mop, vacuum cleaner, a scrub brush, and a Magic Eraser, Lila went to work. It took her five hours to clean the master bedroom and bathroom alone. The thought of what might have occurred in those rooms, and who might have used her things, made Lila's skin prickle. The cleansing was symbolic as well as physical. Lila wanted to wash the grime away from L. T.'s cheating.

After tackling her bedroom, Lila moved to the kitchen next, fearing others had touched her counters and cabinets. Imagining foreign hands, especially those of a stripper, touching her food containers, made Lila shudder. Only God knew what germs were carried into her private living space. Or how many times her house was violated by strangers.

After disinfecting the pots and pans, dishes, and utensils, and running them through the dishwasher, Lila started on the outer surfaces and contents of her refrigerator. Lila wiped everything with bleach water first and cleaned everything again with disinfecting wipes.

Exhausted, drained, and still feeling dirty after cleaning for nine hours, Lila entered her shower just after sunset. She scoured her body with a loofah, scrubbing harder than she ever had before. If only she could wash every cell of L. T. off her skin.

When Lila stepped out, dripping water on the rug, a sense of grunginess clung to her like honey. After dressing, she put a calendar reminder—"Call carpet cleaning company"—in her phone for the next day. Maybe professionals could accomplish what Lila had not—purifying her home from the impure acts of her husband and his mistresses.

That night, Lila locked every exterior door and window and double-checked that each was secure. She also closed the deadbolt she installed on the door to her bedroom.

In addition to everything else she now knew about L. T., that million-dollar policy weighed on Lila's mind.

REFUSING TO PANIC

When trust is broken, it can make us feel as if demons and danger lurk around every corner. Paranoia can replace confidence in everyday matters we previously took for granted. We don't want to be made fools of again, and we need to protect ourselves, so we often overcorrect, taking what someone else did out on every human being who crosses our path.

We should exercise caution, so we don't make an innocent person pay for someone else's guilt. We cannot assume or project another person's wrongdoing onto every encounter. Worrying about what someone might do without merit does nothing but waste time and decrease the quality of our own lives. Because one person hurt and/or betrayed us, does not mean others will automatically do the same.

Basing your perceptions of people and circumstances solely on painful events from your past is like playing a game of chess focused only on capturing the king. If you don't look at all the possibilities, you can set yourself up to experience what you fear—your king getting captured. Sometimes, the smartest strategy is to stay on task and watch the other person destroy himself.

However, healthy boundaries and sometimes even healthier separations are necessary. If danger is present, take whatever actions are required. Without delay. While you do this, pray for wisdom, and ask God to show you the right moves.

Do not be anxious about anything, but in every situation, by prayer and petition, with thanksgiving, present your requests to God. And the peace of God, which transcends all understanding, will guard your hearts and your minds in Christ Jesus.

—PHILIPPIANS 4:6–7

CHAPTER FOURTEEN

STRATEGIES

*Change your thoughts and you
change your world.*

—NORMAN VINCENT PEALE

*L*ila awoke with a raging headache, throbbing muscles, and every nerve in her body feeling like it was ready to snap any second. Sleep had mostly evaded her because of the never-ending scenarios playing in her mind. If there was a way to imagine L. T. ending her life, Lila probably envisioned it. She rolled over in time to catch the blinking light on her cell phone. A message on the screen read:

Are you available to meet me for tea this morning?

Lila waffled on whether to say yes or no. She hadn't talked to her friend Billie since before L. T. moved out. But a cup of hibiscus tea with a friend sounded refreshing. She typed:

Yes. I can be at Panera's in 45 minutes. Will that work?

Perfect. See you shortly.

After exchanging pleasantries, Billie got right to the point. "I ran into our friend Tiffany yesterday, and she told me you and L. T. are getting a divorce. I realize that's probably why you wanted to sell your ATVs. I feel awful about not staying in better contact. I had no idea you were going through something like this."

Lila brushed her hand in front of her face, as if waving off Billie's guilt. "I'm fine. I know you're busy. And I haven't reached out either."

"How are you holding up?"

Lila chuckled. "Do you want my real answer or my public-face response?"

"We're better friends than that. You know I want the down and dirty truth."

"Honestly, most of the time it feels like a lion is breathing down my neck, like he's ready to pounce at any moment. I'm on guard constantly. Even when I'm at work or home alone, I find myself acting like a frightened child. I realize I've developed a habit of questioning myself and tensing up, ready for L. T. to yell at me over the slightest misstep. The fear and anxiety get worse at night. I lock every door and window and find myself obsessively triple and quadruple checking to make sure I didn't miss anything."

"Oh, I can relate," Billie said. "I don't claim to know exactly what you're going through, but from what I experience through my husband's struggles, I understand the battle. Bradley fights anxiety every single day."

"Bradley does? But he's one of the bravest guys I know. He drives a potential firebomb down the freeway, for crying out loud." Lila pursed her lips.

Billie laughed. "I know, but one of the things I've learned is our mental health doesn't always seem reasonable to people looking in from the outside. Bradley suffers from anxiety that nearly debilitates him at times, yet, driving that fuel truck puts him in his happy place."

"Driving a potential explosive is his happy place?"

"It doesn't make sense on the surface," Billie said. "But when you think about it more deeply, it kind of does. He's been driving semi trucks since he was ten years old, when his father first started placing him on his lap and his hands on the wheel. Thirty-eight years later, he feels most comfortable, safe, and confident in the seat of a loaded diesel than anywhere else. He knows the feel and rhythm of big rigs. Ya know, like a NASCAR driver knows the vehicle nuances that can take them across the finish line."

"I never thought about it like that," Lila picked up her tea and took a long sip.

"Bradley feels safe in the cab of his truck. He says he has church while driving and has complete freedom and peace when he talks to God there."

"I could see that," Lila said. "And how do you deal with his anxiety? Where is your safe place?"

"Outside in nature, especially when I'm exercising. Breathing in fresh air and spending time alone with God is my happy place. I can talk to Him about anything on my walks. He's taught me to worry less and trust Him more. My relationship with God frees me to give my husband his own space." Billie took a sip of her coffee. "If it's driving that firebomb as you call it, then I've realized it's between him and God, so I'm all for it. And it's been a weird blessing to deal with Bradley's anxiety issue for another reason. It also helped me come to terms with some abuse in my own past."

"I'm so sorry," Lila said. "I had no idea."

"It happened a long time ago, in my childhood. I mostly buried my memories of it," Billie said. "Or at least I tried to. But the more Bradley's anxiety attacks happened, the more my old memories started bubbling up on me. It was getting harder and harder to repress them."

Billie took another drink. "I finally gave in and let myself remember what I'd tried so hard to forget. The more I faced my past, the more I began to recall. And my memories didn't just contain painful parts. I realized I had buried really great times along with what had hurt me. A lot of joy was lost because of the wounds I worked so hard to avoid. It took me a while to process through with a Christian therapist's help, but I feel so much freer and happier because I did."

Lila wanted the freedom and happiness her friend described and displayed. She did not want L. T.'s abuses to keep her fear-ridden, chronically anxious, paranoid, or to make her bitter. "I'm curious. How did you work through your past without getting overwhelmed by your feelings?"

"Therapy helped tremendously. I also read great books and listened to some good podcasts. And for me, reading my Bible and prayer provided the biggest key. By putting all those pieces together, I was able to create a customized healing protocol for myself." Billie paused, took a sip of her drink, and continued. "For instance, I learned that the part of our brain where abuses are stored is also where the creative side of our thinking resides. This is why people find so much relief through music, drawing, writing, singing, painting, sculpting, or other artistic endeavors."

Lila nodded and wondered if she might end up in therapy again.

"In that common part of the brain, you can switch from a focus on how you were hurt to concentrating on how you will heal. Even developing your own exercise or physical fitness program activates that part of your brain. I'm just beginning this phase of my healing approach now."

"That's fascinating," Lila said. "I've never heard that our creative thoughts are stored with our abuse memories before."

"It's really powerful."

I'm not musically inclined although I do love music. I wish I could hold a tune. But I am interested in exercise and physical fitness. I always wanted to get into really good shape and on a regular fitness regimen, but L. T. never allowed me to do that. Working out also helps me control my stress. This is something I can do now, and I should. I'm ready to shake off my chains and start living like a free woman.

Billie snapped her fingers.

"What?" Lila shook her head.

"Where are you?"

"Here. Go on."

"Like I was saying, I'm a pretty strong extrovert, and I've been made to feel badly about that part of my personality since—well—forever." She shrugged in a "what's new" fashion and laughed.

Billie became serious. "But therapy and prayer taught me to accept myself for who I am. What some call annoying, others see as interesting or helpful. I can work on reigning myself in when I get too over the top without believing I need to hide all of me. I know I talk a lot, and some have told me I never shut up. But it is not true that I never shut up. I can listen well too. Especially when I concentrate on it. Sometimes, I need to hear what someone says about me, and sometimes, they just have a distorted view. I have to look at each case and figure out the appropriate response."

"I've certainly never thought you talked too much." Lila smiled. "I like listening to you."

"Thank you, I appreciate that," Billie said. "Bradley cheerleads me like that. He has been so supportive. Recently, I told him I shouldn't talk so much, and he told me, 'No, don't change who you are.' I know I can get on his nerves, but he loves me anyway. We accept each other, annoying habits and all."

"Must be nice. L. T. always yelled at me for speaking to people when we went out. Even if it was employees of the businesses we frequented." Lila immediately regretted sharing that.

"I'm so sorry," Billie said. "How insensitive of me to gush about my husband when you are going through such a hard time with yours. There goes my mouth again."

"No, I'm sorry," Lila said. "I'm happy for you. I truly am. I didn't mean that the way it sounded. What I mean is that I'm sure it is nice, and frankly, I want to get to a happier place in my life, like you. I don't even recognize myself anymore. I feel so afraid and indecisive."

"You can't change L. T. or his behaviors. He has to answer to God for his actions, and he will. But you work on you. Figure out who Lila is. What does Lila want? What makes Lila happy? I know you are someone who mostly focuses on helping other people, and that's admirable, but you can't help others if you don't help yourself first. Stop apologizing for being you. Pray, and listen for God's voice and His guidance. He will speak to you."

"I am working on me, but I'm not helping anyone like I should right now, not even my kids. I'm not the mom I want to be." Lila sat up straight. "However, there is one bright spot."

"What's that?"

"I do know I'm happier because I don't have to cover for L. T.'s rudeness. I feel a huge pressure lifted off me. The other day, a parent from a kids' team I used to coach told me everyone thought L. T. was arrogant and narcissistic. They associated me with him and gave me a hard time because of him." Lila laughed. "She was one of those parents I struggled with back in the day."

"How sad."

Lila rubbed her temple. "I sure don't know who I am. One minute I feel like I'm gaining strength and going to be OK, and then, all my confidence crumbles. I'm a catastrophe." Lila pulled a tissue out of her purse to catch fluid starting to flow from her nose. "I'm no good to anyone in this state."

"I disagree," Billie said softly. "You are helping someone who needs you more than anyone else right now. You are helping you. You can't see it yet because you are too close to the situation, but I can see you have already taken a few steps on your healing path."

"You're right. I do not see that." Lila sniffled.

Billie grinned. "I have an idea. Would you consider being my workout buddy and accountability partner? There's no pressure. You could take a few days to think about it. Consider starting with a little creative inspiration, like reading a book or listening to a podcast, and decide how you want to approach a fitness regimen. Then we can pick a date to start being accountable to each other, and possibly begin some exercises together. What do you think?"

Lila felt torn. A part of her wanted nothing to do with answering to someone or potentially exposing more failures. Taking on any additional activity also felt overwhelming. But she also knew she stood at a crossroads. Whatever decision she made in this moment would shape her life over the next months or possibly years. If she gave in to her feelings, she could be just as stuck ten years in the future. But if she started making transformational changes, she might finally find the freedom that eluded her.

"Deal." Lila got up and hugged her friend. "It's time for a happier, healthier new me."

"Awesome. This is going to help me too," Billie said. "You can make sure I stay on track."

Something Lila hadn't experienced in a long time spread over her face—a big, authentic grin.

"Thank you for agreeing to meet." Billie smiled and picked up her teacup. "Let's make a toast. To renewing friendships and getting better together."

Their cups clinked, sealing the commitment.

Lila marveled that again she hadn't wanted to meet a friend but was glad she did.

Driving to the office afterward, Lila reviewed recent events in her life. Her problems hadn't changed, but it seemed as if an outside force was sending different people with similar messages and guidance to encourage and prompt her to positive action. The notes in her phone were multiplying.

When Lila pulled into the office parking lot, she made a fresh resolve to provide excellent patient care her goal, with her whole heart. She vowed to no longer let anyone make fun of her for "being overly outgoing or friendly."

That night, Lila dropped onto the couch a few minutes after 9:00 o'clock. Temptation told her, "You've had a long day. You can start tomorrow." But the determination growing in her spirit said, "Your days of procrastination are over. It's time for actions, not empty words."

Lila listened to the determination. Billie was right, it was time for a reset. Renewed faith. Fresh determination. And no more apologies for being the person God intentionally handcrafted when He made her.

She clicked on the notes and outline she'd created in her phone over lunch. "No moment like this one."

She started by listening to her first self-development podcast, one Billie recommended. Lila wrote notes furiously, attempting to capture every detail and each thought that crossed her mind while the host spoke. Midway through the first episode, she had to hit pause when something the speaker said triggered an old memory. Lila documented the details and recognized the event had impacted her deeply.

I was the only student in my eighth-grade class to get all A's, because I was the only student, girl or boy, to get an A in industrial arts.

Even though most girls didn't enjoy this required class, I loved it. The intricate details of labeling the architecture drawings made me happy.

A few weeks after class started, I chose to make a lamp for an assigned project. I had to curve the metal for the lamp base using a machine that I guided by hand. Then I riveted it together and even wired it all by myself with my teacher's gentle guidance. I remember how proud I felt the first time it lit up after I plugged it in. That lamp was probably my first major accomplishment.

My instructor told me I should enter the lamp into a contest, so I did.

I'll never forget the day of the judging. Mom came. We stood near my lamp, and I whispered, "There aren't any other girls here."

In her most matter-of-fact tone, my mom said, "So?"

That day, I learned success didn't care if I was a girl or boy. I won a first-place blue ribbon and a certificate. I could do whatever I wanted or anything that interested me, even if it wasn't the norm. I could be successful in whatever I liked. Living with L. T. made me forget I knew that.

But something else jumps out at me about winning that contest. Even though I was nervous when I first entered the classroom, I came to love industrial arts. Today, I can fix most things myself because of what I learned in school and from watching other people work. I am a better person because I overcame my fears. But I did let one thing hold me back.

As much as I felt passionate about designing and building, I didn't want to be an architect. My dad was one. I allowed that bias to stop me from doing something I enjoyed.

Penning the last two sentences broke Lila's internal dam, allowing decades of unresolved grief to spill out. She mourned the loss of her father, but she also mourned the loss of opportunities missed. Instead of shoving her feelings away this time, she let them pour out, and by doing so, it didn't take long for her to recall something else she'd buried—her last conversation with her father before he died.

They hadn't spoken in years when he called. He was in town to attend a class reunion, but he acted as if they talked regularly and pretended Lila was the reason for his visit.

Lila had responded swiftly and boldly. "You're only in town to go to your reunion."

"You're a !@#$% little !@#$%."

"You can call anyone that but not your own daughter!" Lila shouted into the receiver. She hung up without waiting for more. Those were the last words they exchanged.

Sitting on her living room couch, Lila cried over the event that happened twenty-five years ago. But something unexpected eventually came to mind.

Lila realized she was able to handle her emotions, and her tears quickly dried. Where she'd avoided memories like this one before, because she assumed the pain would be greater than she could bear, she found giving her feelings space lightened her heaviness.

Reveling in her breakthrough, Lila thought about finishing the podcast. But she didn't want to tackle too much too soon. Instead of pressuring herself to do more that night, she made it her goal to complete one emotional exercise a week. She could listen to the rest of the podcast in a day or two.

That night, Lila slept well and woke up refreshed. After Grace got on the school bus, Lila sat at the kitchen table and called Billie and told her about the previous night's experience. Lila explained how surprised she'd been to realize that doing what she'd avoided for years made her feel like a new person.

"I'm so happy for you," Billie said, happiness obvious in her voice. "One thing I've learned is that most of what we fear never happens."

"I believe you."

"You've made a great start on improving your mental health, so let's talk about something else. OK, accountability partner?" Billie paused. "I'm not sure it's safe for you to stay in your house alone."

"I think I'm OK now."

"Why don't you and Grace stay with us? At least until you get through the divorce and are sure L. T. isn't going to lash out."

Lila coughed. "I appreciate the offer—I really do—but I don't want to uproot Grace. This is the only home she's known. And I am taking precautions. The private detective I hired is keeping a close eye on L. T."

"That's great, but he can't watch him 24/7," Billie said. "I just want you to stay safe. And I don't want to have to do an intervention to protect you from danger—or your own stubbornness." Billie's laugh signaled her return to humor.

"I'll be fine. But if I think anything about my safety is changing, you will be the first to know. OK, boss?"

"All right," Billie said.

When they got off the phone, Lila considered Billie's concerns. L. T. had proven his low regard for her and their children's feelings. His goal seemed to be to torture Lila and destroy everything she had. And yet, Lila couldn't shake a secret thought.

No matter how many wounds L. T. had inflicted on her, Lila still wanted her husband to put his arms around her and hold her. She wished he would tell her the past couple of months were a bad dream and everything would be OK. Lila stopped herself midstream.

At that moment, she realized she was one of those abused women who wanted her perpetrator to love and accept her, even if it meant sacrificing all of herself to achieve it. The epiphany made her muster every bit of will that she could find inside herself.

To the empty chair next to her, she said, "I have let L. T. squelch my spirit long enough. No more. I have lost my true self trying to make other people happy, but that ends today. I am not defined by other people's abuse. I can be a gracious, kind, gentle woman who is also confident, strong, and courageous. This is who I choose. I choose me."

Now Lila hoped she had what it took to stand firm. She would start by getting her dog back.

TAKE THOSE THOUGHTS CAPTIVE

Do a quick analysis. Have you often felt or expressed guilt, embarrassment, or shame for who you are? If so, today is your day to say, "No more." It's time to embrace the wonderful, beautiful, and amazing human being whom God invested so much personal care in creating.

Stop apologizing and celebrate you. Your quirks represent your uniqueness. Your differences from others stand for your contributions. Your mistakes, flaws, and failures provide learning lessons for you and others. And guess what? We all have them.

When your brain tells you there is something wrong with you, take those thoughts captive. Renew your mind by finding out what God says about you, His child, in the Bible. Then focus on His truth versus emotional illusions. Write scriptures down that speak about God's love for you. Keep them in key places for reference when you feel low. Sure, we all need continual improvement, but humbly working to overcome your weaknesses does not have to mean giving up your very essence.

And if it's been a while (or never), give yourself permission to express delight. Dance again. Sing out loud. Play more. Allow yourself to feel past pain that also releases previous joys. Find that younger version of you who loved freely and lived passionately, the person before the hurts. Embrace her and invite her back into your life.

Become intentional about cultivating, reinstating, or maintaining healthy friendships. Have one friend who won't sugarcoat when a hard truth is called for, though she always delivers with love. That true friend who isn't just there for you when things are going wrong or are bad, but she's the first to express happiness for you when things are going well. She doesn't gossip with you, so you know she doesn't gossip about you. The friend you support and celebrate with when she needs it, and who gives it right back when the tables turn. She's not afraid to say, "I'm so sorry you're going through this," but she's equally quick to exclaim, "I'm so happy for you."

If you find yourself groaning and moaning that you don't have a friend like this, pray and ask God to bring that amazing soul into your life. Open your heart, eyes, and ears. He will deliver, but you need a willingness to see what He's offering.

And don't be surprised if He doesn't nudge you to make the first move in striking up a conversation with someone new. God creates opportunities, but we still have to take action in alignment with His will.

If your friendships are toxic, and you see this truth, gently, lovingly, but firmly begin to change the relationship, if possible. If the other person is not willing to remove the venom from your interactions, it might be time to move on. It is always appropriate to love, but some people are better loved from a distance for the sake of all involved.

Remember, if you are giving up, or have already given up, and are isolating from the world, something is wrong. It's time to capture those thoughts, get out, and begin living again.

Do not conform to the pattern of this world, but be transformed by the renewing of your mind. Then you will be able to test and approve what God's will is—his good, pleasing and perfect will.

—ROMANS 12:2

CHAPTER FIFTEEN

FACE-OFF

By failing to prepare, you are preparing to fail.
—BENJAMIN FRANKLIN

A couple of months later, as Lila walked up the courthouse steps, L. T.'s words kept running through her head. "I'm getting everything—the kids, the house, our businesses, everything. No one likes you. You will have nothing. No one."

When the hearing began, L. T.'s attorney immediately demanded an independent custody evaluation by accusing Lila of child abuse. He claimed that by giving her children vitamins and driving fast out of their driveway, she was intentionally inflicting harm.

Lila felt sure the judge would see how ludicrous those examples were. But when the next accusation came, she did worry. Lila flashed back to one of her greatest regrets.

A few months earlier, they were in the kitchen when Lila fell for L. T.'s trap. He stood next to their son and repeatedly encouraged Heath to talk back to Lila.

Any statement Lila made triggered a rebuttal from Heath at his father's subtle urging. L. T. stood in silence, with lips upturned into a self-satisfied smile. He took particular pleasure when Heath not only spoke disrespectfully and rebelliously to his mother but started calling her names.

Lila reacted to the name calling without conscious thought. She slapped Heath. But instantly wished she could take it back.

It didn't escape Lila's attention that L. T.'s smirk transformed into a big grin. She stared at her husband. *Why doesn't he tell our son to respect his mother?*

In court, Lila knew the answer. L. T.'s plan had worked. He'd gotten her to react and could legitimately accuse her of striking one of their children. On this basis, all parties agreed to L. T.'s demand for the independent custody evaluation, which would take two months to complete.

Lila's attorney leaned over. "All but seventeen percent of moms get their kids. You will be fine." But Lila wasn't fine. With each passing day, Lila became more and more anxious about the report.

When it came by express delivery, Lila ripped the envelope open with trembling hands. It took several minutes for her brain to register that the evaluation results placed her in the seventeen percent category. Lila had lost her children. She fell to her knees and wondered how she could continue living without seeing her children every day.

She continued reading on the floor. The evaluation laid out a disturbing plan. Only because L. T. didn't want Grace, the judge decided she could live with Lila full-time. Though he ordered Heath to spend a few allotted days with Lila, all nights were with his father.

Lila panicked. L. T. is out all night with different women. He won't even be home with Heath at night.

She had prayed so hard and didn't understand why God would not let her have both of her kids. She struggled to breathe. "Why God? Why God?" Lila cried out.

Gasping for air, Lila told herself, "Stop worrying. Pray." She focused on Philippians 4:6, mentally repeating the passage. "Do not be anxious about anything, but in every situation, by prayer and petition, with thanksgiving, present your requests to God." She rocked on her knees in silence, waffling between fear and doubt, and faith and hope.

Several minutes later, a quiet voice spoke in Lila's spirit. *Let me take care of them. It is out of your hands.*

Lila let the message sink in and prayed out loud. "I give them into your hands. Please take care of my babies. Please give me the strength to not worry myself sick. Help me to breathe and stop panicking. Protect them and help me get both of them back."

Still scared but breathing easier, Lila stood and wiped the tears from her swollen face. She resolved to fight for her children, even if Heath did not want her in his life. She knew he needed to know that his mama loved him, regardless of how he treated her.

From that point on, day after day, Lila spoke Philippians 4:6 over her situation. She posted the verse on her bathroom mirror as a daily reminder. After a few weeks, Lila recognized that allowing herself to mourn but not stay stuck in her grief was one more mental step in the healing direction. She might feel fear, but she refused to let it consume her.

Six months passed, and yet another hearing date approached. Much had changed, while some things stayed the same.

Lila had bare-knuckled until she made the medical practice operational again, though she now practiced solo. Grace was doing well and continued to live with Lila. Heath still lived with his dad. She didn't think his therapy was helping much, but it did allow Lila the opportunity to see her son in an environment designed to help them hear each other. And she'd finally negotiated Sammy's return.

In preparation for court, Lila worked with Roberts and Bansmith to gather all the evidence possible. In their last meeting, Bansmith had said, "I know I never want to go up against you." Roberts agreed.

On April 10, Lila walked up the courthouse steps with her chin held high, knowing she'd done her best to prepare. Now, the outcome rested in the judge's hands.

While waiting for their case to be called, Lila's mind whirred. *No matter how things turn out, at least one day I can tell both my children I gave everything I had to fight for them.*

Several friends, including ones from her Bible study group, sat in the courtroom to show support. When L. T. saw the number of people there for his wife, an unreadable expression crossed his face. He looked like he'd been caught.

But two people were missing—the two attorneys.

The lawyers finally arrived together, coming through the door leading to the judge's chambers. Each walked to their respective tables and motioned for their clients to join them.

Judge Calvin entered the courtroom.

The bailiff cleared his throat. "All rise for the honorable, Judge Thomas Calvin."

When the formalities were complete, the judge sat at his bench, identified the case number and litigant names for the court stenographer, and opened the proceedings. "After speaking to counsel for both parties, I understand an agreement has been reached for custody of the minor children."

What? Lila looked at her attorney who put up his forefinger to signify patience.

Judge Calvin directed his attention to L. T.'s lawyer. "Mr. Lewis, would you like to open?"

L. T.'s attorney spoke rapidly. "My client has agreed to let his wife have primary custody of the children. He also agrees that the children may live with her."

Lila wondered if she heard correctly. *What did he just say? Did L. T. just give me the kids without a fight?* She leaned toward her attorney and started to whisper, but he shushed her.

L. T.'s attorney added, "Based on the revised custody evaluation, my client has no objections to the psychiatrist's opinion." He sat, apparently having said all he wanted.

Thank you, Lord, Lila praised silently.

"May I have a moment to confer with my client, your honor?" Roberts said.

"You may," Judge Calvin said.

Lila's attorney leaned close. "In the judge's chambers, I found out the court-appointed psychiatrist submitted a revised custody report. It was entered into evidence this week. Recommendations changed based on L. T.'s numerous relationships, including his living with a woman while married to you. I also think his newest lover is averse to having your children around."

Two emotions swirled inside Lila for her kids: excitement and pain. How could L. T. just give them up like that? Lila didn't care much about the rest of the proceedings, whether she got a dime, the house, or any of their business. Her children would live with her under one roof. Her prayers were answered. But how would Heath like the new arrangement?

After her excitement died down, Lila sat through the additional testimonies, mostly related to their finances.

After some preliminary haggling, Lila's attorney presented first. "Your honor, Dr. Leroy Frost, the husband in this matter, has repeatedly broken his marriage vows, as evidenced by exhibits A through K."

The judge pushed his glasses up his nose and read from the computer monitor in front of him. He nodded slightly while he scanned what Lila assumed were the eyewitness accounts, purchase receipts, banking and credit card statements, private investigation reports, and more documentation submitted prior to the hearing. Without looking away, the judge said to Mr. Roberts, "Continue."

The attorney nodded. "My client, also a doctor in her own right, has evidence of at least five recent mistresses, one of which is a stripper mister Dr. Frost now resides with."

"Objection," L. T.'s attorney shouted. "My client's current girlfriend no longer works in that industry."

Judge Calvin put his finger on the computer screen as if holding his place, eyed L. T.'s lawyer, and turned toward Lila's table. "Mr. Roberts, will you concede to changing your terminology to former stripper?"

Hushed giggles boomeranged throughout the gallery.

Roberts said, "We have no objection to that change, your honor." He paused a few more seconds to let the echoing laughter die down before continuing.

Lila's attorney picked up a few pages off the table and waved them for emphasis while he spoke. "In addition to transcripts and other proof that highlights his marital infidelities, we can show that mister Dr. Frost has also caused emotional distress to my client through other betrayals. Exhibits L through S expose how he locked her out of shared accounts. He removed business computers that hindered her medical practice. He changed missus Dr. Frost's home security codes without her prior knowledge. He also paid jointly held debts late after agreeing to take responsibility for those expenses."

The attorney took two steps forward while his voice ramped up. "For seventeen years, prior to mister Dr. Frost's insistence in taking exclusive control of the finances, missus Dr. Frost capably handled the bookkeeping for their medical practice, as well as their personal household. And she never paid an additional red cent for all that diligent, hard work."

Roberts took a dramatic breath while he stepped back toward the table. He gently laid a hand on Lila's shoulder and lowered his tone. "In those seventeen years, there is no recording of past due payments or late fees on even one Frost account. And yet, in the months since their separation and mister Dr. Frost's financial control, over $260 in late fees and $430 in overdraft charges were incurred across several accounts. The office utilities were shut off twice."

Lila wanted to look at L. T., but followed her attorney's advice to avoid eye contact.

"Now, my client's previously crystal clean credit score has multiple dark stains. And to add insult to her injuries, mister Dr. Frost, who insists he has no funds to help support the care of their young daughter, has paid a CPA over $9,800 in a matter of months for work my client could have done at no cost. His actions are ruining her credit and demeaning to her reputation. I ask you to consider the copies of bills, statements, emails, and texts in our filed documents."

Roberts slowed his cadence. "Your honor, we humbly request that you review the mountains of evidence pointing to my client's respectable conduct, in the face of her husband's aggressive and passive-aggressive behaviors. She has repeatedly put the interests of her children, her patients, and her community ahead of her own. She has not retaliated or tried to seek revenge, even though it would be understandable under her circumstances. We ask that you find for my client's petitions, not just for her good, but so mister Dr. Frost learns that taking advantage of people has serious consequences." Roberts walked behind Lila and took his seat.

"Anything else, Mr. Roberts?" Judge Calvin said.

"No, your honor."

The judge turned and addressed L. T.'s attorney. "Mr. Lewis. Would you like to present your case?"

"Yes, your honor." The lawyer stood. "My client is a doctor in good standing who loves his family and, though he's made mistakes common to a lot of imperfect people, remains an upstanding citizen. His children are willing to forgive him for his minor indiscretions," the attorney turned and gave Lila a piercing look, "even if his wife is unwilling."

Lila's face flushed as she fought the impulse to stand and shout in defense of herself. Did he seriously just call L. T.'s actions minor indiscretions?

L. T.'s attorney shot her a smug look before turning to face Judge Calvin again. "My client also has concerns about his wife's controlling ways."

Lila quickly caught herself before the scowl formed on her face. She stiffened and remembered her lawyer's counsel before they arrived. "Display the same level of dignity under the judge's scrutiny that you've shown publicly—in spite of your husband or his attorney's behavior." Lila bit her lower lip.

L. T.'s attorney continued. "Dr. Frost is concerned with Mrs. Frost's—"

"Objection, your honor," Roberts said. "My client deserves equal respect and acknowledgement of her status as a physician. Could you please advise opposing counsel to refer to her as missus Dr. Frost? Just for clarity?"

"Certainly," the judge said. "I understand the confusion that comes from both spouses carrying the title of doctor, however, Mr. Roberts is correct. The respect shown to one should be equally shared with the other. Please continue, Mr. Lewis, but use the proper title for each litigant."

Lewis cleared his throat before restarting. "And finally, your honor, my client asks for the court's mercy regarding his financial challenges. He is doing his best to keep up with everything, despite newly learning the extent of his business indebtedness while dealing with his wife's bitterness and fits of rage."

The judge's nod was nearly imperceptible.

Does this mean he believes all of L. T.'s lies and sympathizes with him? She swallowed hard and willed her emotions down. *Hang on to the positive. He did not get away with taking your children. Wear your game face*, she reminded herself. And she repeated John 8:32 from the Bible to herself: "The truth will set you free."

Judge Calvin pulled Lila from her thoughts with a simple question. "Mr. Roberts, would you like to call your first witness?"

"Yes, your honor. I'd like to call private investigator Mr. Marc Bansmith."

Lila glanced toward L. T.'s table. Her husband was not happy with this witness. Lila was sure he never thought her smart enough to hire a PI.

Bansmith's testimony took more than two hours between the amount of testimony he had to give and the number of objections raised. As Roberts had predicted, the investigator made L. T. look more fool than foe. Not only was Bansmith a viable witness, but he had documentation to support the marital infidelities, L. T.'s workplace harassment and emotional abuse of employees, along with multiple financial breeches of trust.

Lewis's cross-examination was brief and weak. When it was over, Bansmith winked at Lila on his way to the back of the courtroom. But his reassurance didn't help her nerves much. She was next.

Looking at his watch, the judge said, "It's nearly noon, folks. Let's recess for lunch, and resume at 1:00 p.m." He tapped his gavel lightly and excused the room.

Lila needed a break. She had several questions to ask her attorney.

Over hamburgers, pickles, and chips, Lila grilled Roberts. "Why did you allow L. T.'s lawyer to make me look so bad? Why didn't you object when he called me controlling?"

"Too many people today believe winning a battle means openly waging war in a fight to be right. They want to shout from every platform possible in attempts to defend themselves and to look better than others. They throw words around like hand grenades, blowing up relationships and, frankly, their real opportunities to win."

Lila nodded and munched on a chip.

"You see, it's much wiser to let facts speak for themselves. Preparing and presenting those facts in the right time, place, and format gains you a lot more credibility. *How* you say something is as important as *what* you say. Actually, it's often more important."

A glint in Roberts's eyes accompanied a spreading mischievous grin. "In a court setting, the one who understands the value in patiently waiting for the right strategic moment to present each piece of evidence, to object, or to argue, usually comes out on top. Often, your best bet is to say nothing at all and let the other side hang themselves by talking too much or making obviously ridiculous claims."

Lila nodded again and took a sip of her drink.

"Like Lewis did when he accused you of abusiveness and excessive control over giving your kids vitamins. You think the judge didn't see through that baloney? And see how things worked out when the psychiatrist reviewed the entirety of the facts. It's best to present your evidence calmly and let the facts speak for themselves. Don't exaggerate. Don't dramatize. And never protest too much."

"I hope you're right."

Roberts furrowed his brow. "He's a judge. He does consider everything, but most of the men and women sitting on the bench got there because of their ability to read and uphold the law. Sure, some have more common sense than others, but I've argued in front of Judge Calvin before. He tends to be fair to both parties."

"Trust is a big ask for me these days."

Roberts chewed a bite of his sandwich and swallowed. He laid a hand on Lila's forearm. "You can't make everyone pay for the wounds one person inflicted on you. At some point, you must release the emotional energy you're giving to what L. T. did to you. Make space for more deserving people. Allow them in."

Lila nodded. Deep down, she recognized that as much as she wanted protection from L. T., she'd also wanted other people to see her as right and him as wrong. She'd spent a great deal of time and energy telling her side of the story and looking for supportive allies. She'd also projected a lot of presumption and assumption onto innocent people in attempts to guard her heart from hurt like her husband had coldly dispensed. But when would she stop allowing the past to rule her present? When would she stop letting L. T. steal her life?

Lila and Roberts spent the rest of lunch focused more on their food than on conversation. As they moseyed back to the courthouse, Roberts reviewed a few pointed questions he planned to ask Lila when she was on the stand.

When her name was called, Lila's heartbeats felt like Morse code ticks, banging rapidly for a few seconds, before stopping altogether, then repeating the frenzied pattern again. Seated in the witness stand, she clasped her hands to try and stop the trembling. She took deep, calming breaths.

Roberts stood in front of her and nodded in a reassuring way.

She remembered another pretrial admonition he'd given her. "When you're on the stand, look directly at the judge and tell only the truth. Stand firm in your conviction that you did not create this situation but show your willingness to cooperate in whatever way will bring the healthiest resolution. And don't forget, we are prepared; you are prepared." Lila nodded back at Roberts.

After verification of her identity and a few indisputable facts about the case, Roberts jumped right to matters of Lila's heart. Roberts held up a blurred photo of her wearing no clothes. Lila recognized one of the mortifying images she'd found online. "I'd like to present this as evidence," he said matter-of-factly. Then to Lila, "Is this you?"

Lila flushed and bit her bottom lip. The humiliation from what LT. had done to her mixed with embarrassment from having it publicly displayed caused her voice to break and her eyes to well up. "Yes, sir."

Roberts softened his tone. "I know this is difficult, Dr. Frost. And I apologize for having to bring up painful memories for you." He offered the disgusting image for her to take and review. "Do you recognize this photo?"

Lila's whisper was barely audible. "I do."

"Please speak up, Dr. Frost," the judge said.

Lila concentrated on projecting her voice in spite of the tightness in her throat. "It's one of the naked pictures my husband took when he drugged me." Lila's heart thumped like a conga drum filling her ears. She was surprised that L. T.'s attorney didn't object.

Roberts paused to let Lila's statement linger in the air. "Dr. Frost, how long had you and mister Dr. Frost been married before you began to notice behaviors that made you feel uncomfortable?"

Lila twisted her left pinkie finger resting on her lap but did not look down. "I noticed his impatience with me right away. It seemed like I couldn't do anything right. L. T. constantly told me I was a bad person because I talked too much or acted too friendly with other people. I remember one time just a few days after we got home from our honeymoon. We were home for lunch. I made the mistake of asking my husband what he wanted for dinner that night. I did not expect his response."

"Oh? What was that?"

"He asked me if I was stupid or something. He said, 'Can't you see I'm home for my lunch hour? I'm trying to relax. Don't you know better than to disturb me?' But I really didn't know any better. I simply wanted to make him something he liked for supper, so I thought asking him was a good thing to do. After that, L. T. had a way of making me feel stupid most of the time, even when he barely raised his voice. He has this smooth way of talking so it makes you feel like you are the one at fault, and then he'll turn around and act innocent as if you imagined what you saw or heard. I don't know how many times he's told me things were just in my head. When you hear that enough, after a while, you begin to believe it, even if someone is lying and manipulating you to get their own way."

"Can you provide an example of that for the court?" Roberts said.

Lila took a long breath and exhaled. "L. T. and I got married in August and I was pregnant by December. When I found out, I fretted all day, worrying about his reaction. What were we going to do? We had no set income. We had no home. We'd just settled on moving here to start our own practice, thirteen hours away from our families and friends back home."

Roberts encouraged her with a nod.

"We'd used protection, but I'd gotten pregnant anyway. We were $200,000 in student loan debt alone, starting our new business. We were broke. I wondered how we were going to eat, much less afford to raise a baby. I worried about what L. T. would say. Would he be mad? Would he want to keep the baby? Would he want me to get an abortion?"

Roberts folded his hands in front of him while Lila continued.

"This was not an option for me. I passionately believe in the sanctity of life, and I have loved my children from the moment

I knew they were in my womb." Lila stopped to allow the heightened emotion in her voice to subside.

Roberts waited.

"When L. T. came home from work, I let him settle into his recliner, then I showed him my positive pregnancy test. I thought he was upset because he didn't respond for the longest time. Then he looked at me with an expression I couldn't read and said, 'Congratulations, Mommy.' I was shocked, and at that time I thought everything was going to be OK."

"Did something happen to change your perspective?"

"Not at first. I was so wrapped up in all the love I felt for this growing baby inside of me and assumed L. T. felt the same way. When I felt Heath move, I couldn't believe we had created a living human being together. Although I was still afraid and our financial future was uncertain, I was so excited to see this little life and to meet him or her in person."

Roberts glanced at the judge and refocused on Lila.

"I concluded that God used my pregnancy to encourage me to take care of myself. So, I decided not to worry as much, for our baby's sake. I mostly succeeded. Except when L. T. would make one of his digs. He did it a lot and they always confused me."

"What kind of digs did he make when you were pregnant?"

Lila shifted in her seat. Old memories rushed to the forefront of her mind. "When your belly grows with your pregnancy, you have to adjust to your body's changes. There's a learning curve, and it can throw your balance off. Once, we went to a restaurant and my foot caught on the chair leg when I tried to sit down, causing me to stumble. L. T. kept his voice low and measured and told me I was an embarrassment. He said it wasn't fair that people looked at him because I was so clumsy."

Lila twisted her pinkie harder. "He also had a habit of pointing out beautiful women, thin and usually younger than me. He seemed to enjoy going into great detail about why he liked their bodies. It was bad enough when I wasn't pregnant, but it made me especially self-conscious when I was."

"I'm sorry you had to endure that, Dr. Frost," Roberts said sympathetically.

"Thank you." Lila looked at L. T. and to the judge. "I tried everything to make my marriage work. I always told myself and my husband I would stay with him as long as he didn't lie to me. Unfortunately, I even broke that vow to myself. I caught him in many lies through the years."

Lila sighed. "I wish I would have had the confidence and self-esteem to leave on my own, but even though L. T. wasn't physically abusive, I later realized he was sexually and mentally abusive. I now see how much fear he perpetuated in me. Living with him, I tiptoed through life, terrified of upsetting him. I never once considered that he didn't care about upsetting me. I don't want either of my children to live with that shadow hanging over their heads."

"Thank you, Dr. Frost," Roberts said. "I have no further questions, your honor."

"Mr. Lewis, you may proceed," the judge said.

L. T.'s attorney stepped forward. He tried to press Lila's emotional buttons with distortions and exaggerations, but she stayed steady and kept her voice calm. For her children's sake she had to maintain composure.

Much quicker than she expected, Lila was excused. Roberts informed the judge that she was their last witness. L. T.'s attorney could now call his witnesses.

The only person Lewis called to the stand was Raven, L. T.'s ex-stripper live-in. She lied repeatedly, even speaking about events she wasn't involved in, but Lila's attorney made short work of her deceptive statements. In his objections and subsequent cross-examination, all he had to do was reference documented dates, times, locations, and other evidence. The platinum blonde's chin quivered often, and she avoided eye contact when she walked past Lila and Roberts after being excused.

At 4:10 p.m., Judge Calvin said, "I will consider all the evidence submitted today and render my decision regarding finances and child support in two months. The next hearing will be on June 24." He typed something on his keyboard before addressing the room with one last statement. "Court is adjourned."

Though the unfinished business of the finances left residual stress, Lila felt much better when she left.

God had given her victory in the most important battle. She'd won her children back.

FIGHTING URGES

When we feel under attack, instinct tells us that we must rise up and defend ourselves. However, this is the time we must exercise great caution and do an honest gut check. Are we truly acting on facts or are emotions driving us to decisions that could cause us greater grief?

It's hard to remain silent when we want to shout for vindication. But if we are constantly battling others in hopes of gaining victory, where does God have a voice or room to work on our behalf? If we insist on screaming, how can others hear the message of truth beyond the lies? If we sacrifice our dignity in the name of anger, when will we be seen for who we truly are?

If you go down the path of over-defense, you empower others to question you. If you make too many excuses, you will appear guilty. This can lead to a place of self-doubt, which can in turn cause you to defend yourself even more, creating a vicious cycle that's hard to break.

The secret to triumph, and inner freedom, comes from courageous confidence in allowing facts and truth to defend us. There is no need to shout when a whisper of wisdom speaks more loudly.

"No weapon forged against you will prevail,
and you will refute every tongue
that accuses you.
This is the heritage of the
servants of the LORD,
and this is their vindication from me,"
declares the LORD.

—ISAIAH 54:17

CHAPTER SIXTEEN

TRANSFORMATION

The first step in achieving your goal is to take
a moment to respect your goal.
Know what it means to you to achieve it.

—DWAYNE "THE ROCK" JOHNSON

*T*wo and a half months would have felt eternal for Lila if she did nothing but sit around and let the minutes gobble up her life. But she was not the same person who passively waited around in hopes of good things finally happening.

Lila had been following a routine designed to create transformational changes in her spirit, mind, and body. She was grateful for that intentionality while she waited for the judge's final determinations.

Lila had worked with her counselor, Grant, to focus on her mental health so she could protect herself from ever marrying someone like L. T. again. Grant helped her grow and learn from her past.

In one session, Grant told her that some women could look at L. T. and see his true nature instantly. "Those women would cross the street to avoid even walking on the same sidewalk as L. T."

Lila laughed. "I want to be one of those women."

"The key is to do more than just listen to what someone says, make sure their actions match their words."

Through Grant's diagnosis of PTSD and coping skills he taught her, Lila became more self-aware. She learned ways to overcome past trauma so she could avoid making choices that might lead to new anxiety-driven reactions.

Lila also met Tiffany once a week for a dose of spiritual mentorship. She tried churches until she found a congregation she wanted to join.

Her new regimen included a start to her day with at least fifteen minutes of Bible reading. Before falling asleep at night, she studied inspirational and personal development books.

During waking hours, Lila watched less TV and filled her mind with more uplifting music, audiobooks, or podcasts while driving, cleaning, or working out. Her spiritual and mental exercises fed her physical fitness goals.

Tiffany also offered insights and tips from her triathlete training. And having Billie as an accountability partner kept Lila on target when she felt like opting out of exercise.

In the early days of making her health changes, Lila developed a workout routine. She set goals designed to encourage her to do regular workouts using an activity tracker app on her phone. She increased her protein, healthy fats, and reduced carbohydrates. She drank a half ounce to an ounce of water every day for each pound she weighed. She eliminated nearly all sugar and processed foods, even foregoing sweet treats for special occasions. Lila also stopped counting or measuring calories and refused to weigh herself more than once a week.

Lila had learned to read her body's true hunger signals and satiated herself with meat and nutritious food. She noticed that as hard as working out was in the beginning, she felt energized after exercising. She also stretched with each workout to help decrease her stress. Lila learned that rest days were as important as workout days. She went to bed early enough to get a full seven to eight hours night's rest and realized the physical activity was improving her sleep patterns.

Sticky notes posted on mirrors, her refrigerator, and even in her car helped reinforce her newfound fortitude to live fully and freely. Lila vowed to never again let someone diminish her light, even herself. This kept her motivated and on task in what had originally felt like a crazy idea. Now that wild dream was carrying her across a finish line she dared only imagine.

As she took care of herself, Lila found that she was better able to care for others, especially her kids. Lila learned to validate her children's feelings and took them to their own counselors. Lila told them she was sorry for hurting them even though she knew it wasn't all her fault.

Lila learned to just keep loving her kids even if it seemed it was unrequited. She planned different activities with the kids and kept loving them even when Heath said he wanted her out of his life. She attended all the kids' activities and cheered them on from the stands. She learned to give them space but still watch over them to try to protect them.

Sometimes L. T.'s voice replayed in her mind, telling her she couldn't work out, was incapable of doing things on her own, and that she was fat. But Lila turned those old mental recordings off. She did things she was afraid to do before. She stopped doubting herself and leaned into her abilities.

By the time the verdict hearing approached, Lila no longer bore the body frame of a middle-aged woman with arms that kept waving when she stopped waving. The new Lila appeared healthy, lean, strong, and toned. She had her mind set on preparing for and participating in long bike rides, like half-century and century rides. Triathlons were the furthest from her mind. She knew she couldn't do them because she couldn't swim that well or that far. Lila no longer allowed herself to become paralyzed by daunting odds or timelines. And people were taking notice. Something else was changing too.

Lila found her voice as she courageously talked to others. She discovered she wasn't the only one going through a tough divorce or hard situation. Even some in her Bible study group were on their second marriages but appeared happy and at peace.

Lila occasionally watched the playful interactions between wife and husband and thought, *I wish I had someone to share my life with, someone I could laugh and cry with.* But she recalled the years of L. T.'s confusing mental torment and told herself, *I don't think I ever want to go through another divorce again. I don't care if I ever marry.* Besides, Lila hadn't joined the study to find a new husband.

Within the safe confines of her small group, Lila discovered clarity about her true value. She learned to look at herself through God's eyes and appreciate the woman He created. She stopped hiding her honest thoughts and opinions and began sharing them openly, though always respectfully. She found that others wanted to hear what she had to say, and they welcomed her outgoing personality. They even enjoyed her hugs instead of admonishing her for them.

Lila learned she had a gift of encouragement and that God gave her chances to use those gifts to help others and glorify Him. She became braver at using her God-given talents and taking advantage of opportunities He placed before her. She received many blessings as a result. Her focus on improving both her inner and outer being also paid off at work.

Her patients loved her confident encouragement, caring compassion, as well as her professional expertise. They constantly told her how she changed their lives. Present and former employees opened up and talked about their frustrations, concerns, and their own fears.

Lila still fought PTSD, especially when a male displayed strong emotions. Her first instinct was to shut herself off from the world and hide, but she finally realized that because someone was upset or angry, it didn't mean she did something wrong or that she was bad. Surrounding herself with people who were positive and who motivated her helped Lila feel stronger.

All this helped prepare Lila for the hearing date. Lila was ready to hear Judge Calvin's decree.

In the courtroom, the judge reiterated his previous declaration when he somewhat followed the opinion of the psychiatrist.

Primary physical custody of both Grace and Heath to Lila. But now, he added visitation for L. T. every other weekend and one day during the week for the weekend when the children weren't with him.

Not exactly what Lila wanted, but she accepted his decision.

When he rendered the financial side of his decision, Judge Calvin split the marital assets down the middle. Numerous contested filings in the future would drag their finances through the legal system for another four years. On this day, however, the divorce was granted, and Lila was awarded $1,200 a month for child support.

After Judge Calvin finished reading his verdict, he had one more directive for L. T. The judge peered over the bench and lasered in on Lila's now ex-husband. With more force than he'd put behind any message previously spoken, the judge said, "Mister Dr. Frost, it is this court's opinion that you have selfishly and maliciously perpetrated egregious acts against your wife that have also brought pain upon your children. You have endangered her well-being in many ways. Frankly, sir, you are undeserving of such a woman."

Judge Calvin pointed at L. T. "My commitment to professional ethics and personal integrity prevents me from telling you everything on my mind. But I will leave you with this: if I catch wind of any additional harm you do to this woman or your children—and you'd better know I have my ways of finding out—be warned. If you hurt them financially, emotionally, or physically, I will come after you with the full force of the law behind me. If you indirectly cross a line that causes them pain, and there is a legal leg to stand on, you will regret the moment you first entered my courtroom. Up until now, your charm and manipulation may have helped you eke by, but those days are behind you. You will not talk your way out of trouble if you wound your family again, especially your ex-wife. I suggest you learn the value of respecting and protecting those you are responsible for versus seeking to destroy them. Do I make myself clear, mister Dr. Frost?"

L. T. nodded. "Yes, your honor."

"I expect I won't hear your name in legal circles again. Correct?"

"You won't, your honor."

"Then court is adjourned." Judge Calvin banged the gavel and concluded the hearing.

Lila could tell L. T. was not happy with the final exchange he had with the judge, but she also knew he heard what the judge said and seriously considered the warning. Months of worry dissipated in a matter of seconds. Lila left behind her niggling concern that L. T. might try to kill her. She was free to begin again.

Lila felt peace with her children under her roof. She knew it would not be easy, but Lila learned to validate Heath and Grace while she practiced accepting her own value.

When Heath was living with L. T., his absence made Lila feel as if her son was kidnapped. She knew where he was, but she couldn't do a thing about what happened there. After living with L. T. and his girlfriend, Heath seemed to despise Lila at first. But Lila faithfully went to family counseling with the children and clung to hope, especially Proverbs 22:6, "Train up a child in the way he should go; even when he is old he will not depart from it."

In describing her feelings to Tiffany one day over tea, Lila said, "My kids give me breath and they also take my breath away. They are my main reason for existing. Even when they hate me, I can't stop loving them. It reminds me of something a mother I worked for told me many years ago. I was her kids' nanny. She said, 'Kids show us how much God loves us. Even though we hurt

Him, He never stops keeping our best interest at heart, just like we do with our kids when they hurt us.'"

Tiffany nodded and took a sip of her drink.

"Through my separation and divorce, there were many times where everything felt hopeless. It looked like I had literally lost everything, including my children, but I gripped my faith like a life buoy. God held on to me in return. The worst was going from a relationship with Heath where one month he gave me a birthday card telling me how much he loved me to being told the following month he didn't want me in his life. Eventually, I had to release my children fully into God's hands. My efforts to save them had proven useless, but letting God fight the battle on my behalf turned things around. L. T. took them away from me for a while, but he could never take God's hand off them."

Tiffany smiled. "We would all do well to remember that."

Lila took a sip of water and put her glass down. "I certainly have a new appreciation for my relationship with my kids. The things that drove me crazy before like a loud house, dirty laundry, an almost constant need to replenish food, or driving the kids to their extracurricular activities? Instead of frustrating me, they bring a smile to my face. My kids and me? We're a family unit now."

Postdivorce, Lila struggled to get out of debt. She sold the medical building to help with her finances, made a budget, and stuck to it. Providing for the children was difficult because L. T. did not pay child support as ordered by the judge. Eventually, as Heath got older, he stepped up and got a job. Their relationship healed, and he even came to appreciate Lila's personality, often joking how his mom never met a stranger.

L. T. exercised his visitation rights for only a month before he left town without telling the kids. He sent birthday and Christmas cards for a couple of years, then even those stopped.

This was the condition of things when Lila was introduced to an acquaintance of mutual friends. He had blond hair, twinkling blue eyes, and stood two inches shorter than herself. Their first meeting started with laughter.

"Oh. Hey. I'm Corey. But my friends call me Cor. You know, like Thor from the movies," he said, grinning.

After that initial introduction, Corey stuck around. He was a kind soul and quickly stepped in as a healthy male role model for Lila's children. He attended Heath and Grace's activities without being asked and became Lila's best friend. They often talked for hours on the phone, and Heath especially liked spending time with Cor.

Occasionally, Lila wondered, *Is this what it means when you complete one chapter and make room in your life to begin a new one?* But she also didn't want to add complications after she'd worked so hard for peace. Life had a way of sending enough chaos Lila's way, without her help. Could Corey really be trusted?

TAKING YOUR LIFE BACK

We often blame circumstances and people for our inability to succeed. Yet, our mindset is usually our greatest enemy. Who cares if someone else says your dreams are crazy? So what if you must sacrifice today for a better life tomorrow? Where is it written that hard means impossible? When do emotions get to supersede desires?

You stand at a crossroads and make a choice before every decision and action. Taking your life back begins with bold action. Accepting your role in your outcomes, taking responsibility, and gripping fortitude can help you release excuses and quit laying down blame. Today is the first day of the rest of your life. You have the power to control your fears instead of allowing them to control you. Only you can execute on the desires and dreams embedded in your heart.

The question is, which way will you go?

For I can do everything through Christ,
who gives me strength.

—PHILIPPIANS 4:13 NLT

CHAPTER SEVENTEEN

NEW
Beginnings

We must be willing to get rid of the life
we've planned, so as to have the life
that is waiting for us.

—JOSEPH CAMPBELL

*W*here L. T. never had the time or inclination to cheer Heath on, as much as he professed his love for his son, this outsider named Corey left work early to quietly sit in the bleachers and show support. Cor wasn't loud and proud about being there, but his very presence shouted genuine affection. He did, however, seat himself right next to Lila and Grace.

During timeouts and halftime, Lila asked polite questions. "Where do you work?"

"I'm a colorectal surgeon," Cor said, laughing. "Don't worry, though. I know all the jokes."

Lila chuckled. Even though he spoke discreetly, and it didn't bother him, she wasn't comfortable discussing that profession. He must have sensed her unease.

"Seriously though." Cor's face became more somber. "I was also the Maryland Army National Guard state surgeon for twenty-seven years. I retired recently as a full colonel. Some of the guys I served with called me Colonel Fury." Cor laughed. "Of course, I am really like Mary Poppins."

Lila scrunched her brow. "How is that?"

"I'm perfect in every way." Corey laughed again.

Lila marveled at Cor's ability to speak freely and show lighthearted emotions so easily. But she refused to let this jokester pull her in too far. She turned her attention back to the court and pretended not to occasionally check Corey out from her periphery.

Corey kept coming to Heath's games when he was able to get off work in time. He also helped transport Heath when she needed help. Lila and Cor often talked on the phone to make arrangements, then the frequency of calls increased and more often than not had nothing to do with the kids. Then, in mid-May, Corey invited Lila and her kids out to his lake house to ride Sea-Doos.

Ten minutes ahead of schedule, Lila pulled up to Cor's place with the kids. Corey was trying to back his Sea-Doos onto the boat ramp. He pulled forward slightly, straightening the trailer behind the truck, then backed slowly toward the ramp. It took about five seconds for the trailer to begin angling sideways away from the truck. Cor grinned nervously at Lila, then pulled forward and aligned the truck and trailer again. He put the truck in Reverse, and this time, jack-knifed halfway down.

"You OK?" Lila asked while he eased forward for what seemed like the tenth time.

"Yep," Corey said with less confidence in his voice. "Just getting my bearings."

She crossed her arms and watched.

For the next twenty-five minutes, Corey unsuccessfully made attempt after attempt. Lila tried to give helpful directions. *He is a retired colonel. He's used to giving directions. Maybe I could get in the truck and back them down while he directs me.*

"Why don't I try? I've never done this before, but I'll give it a shot. You can guide me."

Corey nodded and got out of the truck.

Lila hopped in, straightened the vehicle up, and deftly navigated the trailer down the boat ramp and into the water on her first try. As soon as she put the truck in Park and watched Cor approach, Lila's buried anxiety resurfaced. Old messages played in her head. *He's going to be so mad at me. He's going to blame me because I was able to do what he couldn't. He's going to yell at me.* Lila cowered in the driver's seat and squinched her eyes.

"You're the man!" Cor shouted. "That was amazing. Who knew you were an expert trailer driver?"

Lila relaxed her grip on the steering wheel. "You aren't angry?"

"For what?"

"Because I got the trailer in the water the first time when you struggled so much."

"Aw, I was totally distracted by your beauty, that's all," Corey said jokingly. "That's going to be the story I stick to anyway."

"Oh yeah?" Lila giggled. "My story won't match yours then."

"Ah, but mine is better."

Lila was shocked. He showed no trace of anger. Instead, Corey seemed proud of her accomplishment. He actually praised her. She wasn't accustomed to that. Her pulse quickened.

Soon after, Cor and Lila went on their first date—skydiving. Lila was nervous and afraid, but it was on her bucket list. For a greater sense of security, she told Corey she wanted the biggest guy to be her tandem skydiver. Instead of taking offense, Corey laughed.

When they arrived to sign in, Cor looked at the cute little brunette behind the counter. "You get the big guy. I want her." Corey and Lila laughed together.

She'd never known anyone so freely fun. And he felt completely trustworthy. Lila loved his openness although it made her blush at times.

Lila knew she loved Corey before the day was over. But she didn't let on. She needed to be sure he was as good as he seemed. She already noticed he was kind to others, not just her. She didn't have to worry about him being rude to other people, and she didn't feel like she needed to cover for him. She just needed to see if it was a facade or if these traits would last.

In the months that followed, Lila learned she could consistently count on Cor's good humor and supportiveness. When she mentioned his name, others only had positive things to say about him. She also learned he said nothing but positive things about her. She enjoyed being with someone who was respectful to her face and behind her back.

Cor also wasn't threatened by her gifts or abilities in any way. When she watched a YouTube video and taught herself to remove an ATV starter to have it rekeyed, he congratulated her instead of making a snarky remark.

When she accidentally left the car door open after bringing groceries in on a snowy day, Cor didn't yell at her or tell her she was stupid. Instead, he sat next to her and put his arm across her shoulders. "If that's the worst thing you do, we'll get along just fine."

Lila had never experienced such a calm, caring soul. It took many months before she stopped questioning his sincerity and wondering if Corey was truly as he appeared. She finally realized he bore no ulterior motives. He believed in doing the right thing whether anyone else was around or not. And instead of trying to make her into someone she wasn't, Cor helped Lila become more of who she really was. He did not make her feel objectified; Corey made Lila feel valued and cherished.

After several years of being best friends, Corey proposed on Groundhog Day. Lila's heart swelled when he said, "Women should be destinations, not drive-thrus." He showed no embarrassment at the tears edging his eyes. He switched from being serious to funny with a standard Cor quip. "I chose Groundhog Day, because I figured if I screwed this up, I could keep proposing again and again until I got it right."

Cor had shown respect for Lila's need to heal and learn to trust again, so during years of being best friends they had not even held hands. Over their three-year engagement, Cor displayed gentlemanly restraint many times when Lila gently reminded him that she wanted to "wait to have sex."

He didn't pressure, nor did he tell her she was old-fashioned or call her a prude. He simply accepted Lila and her convictions. He even told her that he admired that she valued herself that much. But he didn't hide his desire or passion for her either. And Corey was just as consistent with Lila's children.

Grace's approval was evident early on. Lila remembered when her daughter was young and said, "I want to be like Corey because he is loose hearted." Lila was confused at first, until she asked Grace what she meant. "Corey loves loosely because he shares his love and isn't afraid to show it."

Cor's loose-hearted love had won them all over, though Heath still guarded a piece of his. Heath considered Corey a close friend, but after the proposal, held back from fully accepting him as his mom's future husband. Corey, however, relentlessly continued to express love and acceptance.

Lila had come to understand that men are either good, strong fathers, or weak, substandard fathers. They are a safe parent or a dangerous one, whether they biologically produce a child or not.

Corey proved good and safe. He influenced Heath and Grace powerfully and positively. His actions matched his words, and his actions matched God's teachings about what a man is supposed to be. Corey didn't flaunt his beliefs. He showed them in regular, daily habits.

Their marriage ceremony was small with only immediate family in attendance. Lila teased Corey and said she married him for his family. They truly embraced her and her children.

With each passing day, the couple's value and respect for each other grew, as did their sexual appetites. Lila had never known desire and delight on this level. It was the first time she didn't feel used. She knew Corey valued her, sexually yes, but in many other ways too.

OUR PLANS VS. GOD'S PLANS

We envision a plan for our lives. Maybe it's a house with a white picket fence set in a nice, quiet neighborhood with 2.5 kids, a dog, and a tall, dark knight in shining armor. But is that God's plan? In *Lila's* plan, her story concluded when she got her kids back. In *God's* plan, that was only the beginning to her next chapter. And her tall, dark knight? He turned out to be short and hairy—and cute.

Corey saw Lila as a destination, not a drive-thru. Which one are you? Do you value yourself enough to be a destination? If you don't see yourself that way neither will anyone else. You have to value yourself before anyone else can value you. (Start today saying the affirmations.) God already values and cherishes you, and He knows everything about you.

Corey paid Lila compliments. Do you value yourself enough to accept compliments? In a healthy relationship, when a friend or spouse makes positive comments about you, don't brush off what they say with comments like "oh, be quiet" or "you're nuts." Say thank you!

Corey treated Lila's children as his own. One of the biggest powers men have is their influence on their children, whether biological or not. He may not be your children's biological father, but he may be a father figure. The difference he can make in their lives is huge. The love of a father gives children security. A true husband also models for his daughter how her future husband should treat her—that she should be valued and cherished—while teaching his son to treat his future wife in the same way.

Corey was not what Lila had envisioned, but Lila saw what true love was through his actions. God's plans are so much better than we could ever imagine for ourselves.

Love is patient and kind; love does not envy or boast; it is not arrogant or rude. It does not insist on its own way; it is not irritable or resentful; it does not rejoice at wrongdoing, but rejoices with the truth. Love bears all things, believes all things, hopes all things, endures all things.

—1 CORINTHIANS 13:4–7 ESV

CHAPTER EIGHTEEN

NEW Chapters

I can wait for life to shape me in whatever manner it chooses. Or I can shape me to make life whatever I choose.

—CRAIG D. LOUNSBROUGH

*S*ix years later, Lila stood toward the back of a throng standing on a lake shoreline. Waves lapped against the shore. People ran in place, hopped, or shook their arms to keep their muscles warm in the dusky dawn coolness. The starting buzzer signaled, and the swimmers propelled their bodies into the water four at a time.

Lila plunged into the sixty-degree lake water. Icy needles penetrated her wetsuit. She repeated her motivational mantras and set her eyes on the first buoy. With each stroke, her mind pleaded for her to quit, imagining fish, turtles, and snakes swirling around her legs. Other swimmers bumped into her and pushed her under the water, threatening to take her out before she reached her first short-term goal. A panic attack came over Lila. She hyperventilated.

The safety crew floated in a kayak about ten yards away. Lila yelled across the water. "Will I get disqualified if I hold onto the kayak?"

The kayak spotter shouted back. "No. That's what we're here for. Just don't make forward movement while you're attached to us, and you won't get disqualified."

Lila did her best to dogpaddle toward the kayak while the kayak paddled toward her. When she clutched the front, she remembered not to kick, so she wouldn't make forward progress because of the watercraft. While catching her breath, another problem presented itself.

Swaying up and down against the boat with the motion of the waves made Lila feel seasick. Her nausea worsened with each swell. A growing panic mocked her. *You can't do this.* But that thought sparked something else.

Lila's determination sprang to action. She dug down to find her other voice and soon used it to silence the naysayer inside her. *I CAN do this. I can do all things through Christ who gives me strength. Dear Lord, help me do this.*

Lila released the kayak and made sure she was several feet away before attempting a freestyle stroke. The motion made her sick, so she dogpaddled again. She mixed a breaststroke with her next dogpaddling attempt, and that worked.

During training, a coach once told Lila, "In a triathlon, what matters during the swim is to just keep moving forward. Don't worry about what your stroke looks like or what stroke you use. Don't get hung up on appearance."

Just like life. Moving forward is the most important thing, not what it looks like or how you get there.

A fresh wave of nausea overtook Lila. She vomited, but she dogpaddled and breaststroked toward the first buoy anyway. Lila decided hell must include treading water and never being able to get out.

When she made it to her first target, Lila savored the feeling for a moment and set her eyes on the next buoy. From there, one small goal and buoy at a time, Lila reminded herself that she didn't have to do this, but she was privileged to participate. This mindset moved her to victory over every fear and obstacle and closer to achieving her ultimate goal—to finish the 1.2-mile swim. Finally, she made it to the end of the swim.

Lila wanted to hug the volunteer who reached out his hand for her to grab at the finish, but she didn't have the energy. She stumbled out of the water, praying, "God, please don't let me pass out."

She reached the stairs leading to the transition area. Lila unzipped her wetsuit while walking. She prayed again. "Dear Lord, please do not let me trip going up these steps." As she trudged to the top of the stairs, her inner "woohoo" wanted to celebrate. The outgoing and charismatic side of herself showed up more these days, but the exhaustion quickly turned her "woohoo" into a feeling of "oh help."

Lila focused on lifting her feet without puking. She didn't want to embarrass herself in front of cheering family, friends, and strangers. She heard Heath say, "Mom doesn't look so good."

Lila exhaled a long breath as she reached T1—the transition area between the swim and the bike. Biking was her haven and her happy place. She'd cycled before she became a triathlete, and Lila loved the confidence and peace she felt in the saddle. Others might be stronger in the swim, but her biking skills and experience helped her catch up. She only hoped she had enough inner fuel left to complete the triathlon.

On a bike, Lila could normally refute her doubts and insecurities. Mastering her self-talk on a bike meant she could master it anywhere.

When her mind questioned, *Can I make it up the mountain? Is this one too hard? Will I fall over because I can't unclip my feet?* She pushed back. *At least try. Climb that hill anyway. Push yourself, even if you feel like giving up or dying. If you fall, you will get back up and start again.*

When she wondered, *Am I going to finish the race? Will I be left behind and not finish in time?* She pushed back. *Your greatest competitor is yourself. Winning means crossing the finish line—forget what anyone else does or what the clock says.*

When fear said, *You can't do this. You won't overcome because you are weak.* Lila mentally shouted back. *Shut up, self-doubt. You're a loser. Get out of my head. I refuse to give up. I won't give in to you. I'm the little engine that could.*

The walk past the bike mount seemed to take forever and she still felt nauseated. But she got on her bike anyway and slowly started to pedal. Trying not to be sick, she narrowed her eyes on a tall pine tree in the distance. When she reached that landmark, Lila homed in on a shadow at the base of the first big hill. After reaching that target, Lila scoured the peak ahead and identified a large oak to shoot for. This leg of the race was brutal.

It didn't take long for a deep burn to settle into Lila's legs and lungs. Thanks to a lot of prerace practice, she meditated on scriptures. Then she mentally repeated empowering affirmations, sung inspirational songs, and recalled anything positive she had accomplished or that someone had ever said about her.

Lila's heart thumped rapidly against her chest while she and the bike climbed. She mentally repeated Philippians 4:13 three times, emphasizing various key words. *I CAN do all things through Christ who gives me strength. I can do ALL things through Christ who gives me strength. I can do all things through CHRIST who gives me strength.*

Lila's labored breathing intensified. *You CAN climb this mountain. I know it hurts, but you are not going to quit. You are going to prove to yourself and every person who ever doubted you that you are worthy of success. Remember how good you felt when you, the only girl in shop class, won that blue ribbon for your lamp? This is going to feel so much better. You are powerful. You are capable. You are an overcomer.*

Near the top, as Lila's searing legs rammed each resistant pedal down in slow, rhythmic motions, she started singing to herself. In her half-dazed state, she combined a song she'd heard with words she made up when she couldn't remember lyrics. The repeating message fueled her with renewed inner strength. "Good God Almighty, I am blessed. You have carried me to the mountaintop, and I am forever grateful. Because of you, I am saved, I am free, I am victorious. Thank you for making me worthy of the climb."

As Lila's exhausted body propelled the bike the last few inches to the top of the mountain, she kept mentally singing. When she reached the peak, it coincided perfectly with her next words. I. Am. BLESSED.

The view at the crest was mesmerizing. The brilliant shades of emerald and hunter green were enhanced by the sapphire and violet sky. The mountain range spread for miles in panoramic beauty. New energy instantly flooded Lila. All body aches subsided.

In that moment, she felt only freedom and soaring joy. Every lush meadow in the valley, mountain ridge in the distance, leafy tree, yellow, purple, or orange flower below her heightened Lila's adrenaline. The cottony clouds and floating birds made her happiness expand. "Thank you, God," Lila whispered. "I AM blessed."

The sense of accomplishment launched Lila into the descent. Pedaling came easier now. She whooshed down the hill at more than forty miles per hour. But she felt no fear. Only peace. As the wind whistled past her ears, Lila shouted, "Woohoo! Woohoo! I did it!" Of course, she still had to *finish* the rest of the fifty-six-mile bike ride.

As exciting as the biking portion was, by the time Lila stopped before the dismount line, she almost fell over from the exhaustion in her legs. She heard her family cheering again. Heath sounded genuinely supportive when he said, "Great time, Mom. You can do it, you're almost there."

She barely caught a glimpse of her son in the rush to begin the final phase of the triathlon. But Lila did take note of Cor's voice. Did he really just sing, "She's got legs, she knows how to pedal them" while cracking himself up?

Lila laughed but quickly shook her distracting thoughts off in T2—the transition area between the bike and the run allowed her and other racers to grab a bite of food and gulp some electrolyte-infused water.

Lila quickly put her running shoes and visor on and trotted off. She tried not to think about how tired she was and the 13.1 miles she had left to cover.

Running was all mental for Lila. When she was twenty-five years old, the most she'd ever run was a 5k. She was a cyclist not a runner. Two and a half decades later, she was attacking the longest distance she had ever attempted, ten extra miles. Again, her brain rebelled.

You can't run for 13.1 miles. You aren't a runner. You're too slow. What if you bonk and hit the runner's wall? How are you going to do this after biking fifty-six miles with four thousand feet of elevation? What are you thinking? Self-doubt flowed freely until Lila snatched those thoughts and tossed them out of her head.

Like she had while biking, Lila repeated Philippians 4:13 to herself. "I CAN do all things." She added her affirmations. "I am a warrior. I am a child of God. I am blessed. When I am at my worst, I am a child of God. When I am at my best, I am a child of God."

After her mental reset, Lila started her playlist in her head. She let herself get lost in the music in her mind. She ran or walked, with little notice of anything but the rhythm of music, her breathing, and the road in front of her. Her only distraction was the cheering of her family when she passed them and friends. That gave her a boost of energy and the strength to keep going.

In the first three miles, Lila felt the resting brick face she wore, where your legs feel like bricks after biking and your face reflects it. But as the finish line came into view, euphoria wiped the stoic look away and replaced it with a wide smile. Most of the competition beat her time, but Lila didn't care.

She'd won. She completed her first Half Ironman before the cutoff time of 8:30 hours. The clock read 7:31 when she crossed the finish line.

In that moment of revelry, Lila oddly remembered when L. T. competed in a Sprint Triathlon and told her she could never complete one. But though he worked out religiously, he'd never taken on the kind of regimen necessary for a Half Ironman. Ironic. She briefly wondered what he would think if he could see her now, but then she quickly thought *Who cares?*

Lila flicked sweaty bangs out of her eyes and straightened her back, nearly doing a superhero pose. Success was by far the sweetest revenge.

Her family rushed to greet her. Grace hugged her wobbly body. Lila's mom took Lila's face in her hands and kissed her perspiration-slicked cheeks. Although Heath resisted hugging his sweaty mother, his eyes glistened when he said, "Mom, I'm really proud of you." She gathered both kids to her chest and gave them a sweaty hug as they all laughed.

The kids cried out together. "Eww. Gross, Mom."

Cor's voice caused her to turn. She smiled at him. "Not bad for a beginner," he quipped.

"Thanks," Lila shot back good-naturedly.

Later that night, still riding high from her accomplishment, Lila couldn't sleep. Sammy had taken over what used to be L. T.'s side of the bed and he lay sprawled across the pillow. She stroked Sammy's fur, and he nuzzled her hand.

After a few minutes, Lila reached for her notebook and wrote, expanding on her thoughts about success being the greatest revenge. Who knew? Maybe she'd write a book about it someday. She laughed at herself, but only half-heartedly. After all, she'd just completed a Half Ironman triathlon.

After penning several paragraphs, Lila yawned. She placed the notebook back on her nightstand and snuggled under the covers and laid one hand on Sammy. She felt contentment, something familiar these days. She avoided thinking about how it had sadly eluded her earlier life.

Even though the future held many unknowns, one thing Lila understood with certainty: she'd started a new and very exciting chapter.

WASTED ENERGY

How many seconds, minutes, hours, days, months, and years do we expend on wasted energy we can never get back? Time spent listening to negativity and lies? Believing we are incapable of things we never dare try. Wallowing in memories and imaginings about the past. Retaliating or seeking revenge for hurts, or at the very least, thinking about it. A lot.

But what if you were to reinvest that energy into healthier endeavors? Instead of listening to self-doubt and self-recrimination, you could set small goals and inch yourself toward hitting a bigger target—one tiny victory at a time.

Setting your mind on thankfulness for people who have helped you keeps hurtful people from maintaining real estate in your mental space. Refusing to participate in gossip or other inappropriate conversations not only reduces drama in your life but also makes room for encouraging, supportive, and enjoyable relationships.

Focusing on a dream, goal, target, or desire until you achieve it feels sweeter than any perceived payback. Let success win your wars.

And God is able to bless you abundantly,
so that in all things at all times,
having all that you need,
you will abound in every good work.

—2 CORINTHIANS 9:8

CHAPTER NINETEEN

FREEDOM,
Fun, Favor

Liberty, when it begins to take root,
is a plant of rapid growth.

—GEORGE WASHINGTON

*A*lmost thirteen years after her divorce, Lila's life barely resembled its former state of unrest. Selling the building where she had practiced medicine covered all her divorce expenses and paid most of the joint debts with L. T.

Renting an office suite felt like going backward at first, but now, Lila liked having fewer responsibilities for the building. She had time to lavish more attention on her patients. This also allowed her to pursue her passions—triathlon training and competitions, and writing.

Through the years, Lila built a comfortable nest egg for herself and her children. After ten years without seeing their father, the kids learned to accept Corey as a friend. Grace had grown into a beautiful, well-adjusted nineteen-year-old young woman who loved Corey as her father figure. But she also accepted her father for who he was. She adored her mom.

Twenty-five-year-old Heath now lived on his own and was thriving at his chosen university, where he studied medicine. Through professional counseling, and consistently exercised unconditional love from Lila, Heath accepted and appreciated his mom more. His relationship with his father was a bit of a roller coaster, but Lila stayed out of it.

Although L. T. had somewhat reentered Heath and Grace's lives after his long absence, he lavished more attention on his current wife's son than his own children. At least that's the way it appeared from social media posts. L. T. had created a new family with Raven, built on their shared narcissism, an unethically run medical practice, and ongoing financial problems, but he did try harder to have a relationship with Heath.

Regardless, Lila had peace. Her faith, friends, and new family helped her leave L. T.'s issues between him and God, where they belonged. Old worries and fretting rarely stole her joy anymore.

Despite L. T.'s attempts, for the most part, Heath had a healthier and more mature perspective of his dad these days anyway. Lila's son came to her house weekly for a family dinner, was less critical, laughed more, and genuinely enjoyed her company. Plus, she had too many other wonderful blessings to focus on.

When her marriage disintegrated, Lila told everyone, including herself, she wanted no part of another romantic relationship. But God not only has a sense of humor, sometimes He's downright hilarious.

When Lila met Corey, his unconventional personality and blunt honesty were equally charming and off-putting to her. Not only was there never a mask worn to impress people, he also obviously cared little about being anything but absolutely true to himself. Yet, with everything she'd been through with L. T., Lila trusted no man and had no desire to get tangled up with another one.

But Cor kept showing up—and showing off—over months that turned into years. And mostly, he didn't even realize he was impressing her. By simply being himself—cool, calm, and quirky—Cor accumulated points in his favor. The way he cared for Heath and Grace and showed up for them melted Lila's heart. He made the kids and her laugh with his fun-loving spirit.

When Lila and Corey returned from their wedding anniversary getaway, a large box waited on the front porch. They carried it inside where Lila opened it with trembling hands. Corey stood back and allowed her to have the moment.

When she pulled the first book out of the box, Lila caressed the cover, and held it out to Corey. This written work represented years of sweat and a nod to their new life.

In recent years, Lila's previously silenced and weak voice had become strong and clear. She openly shared messages of encouragement and influence around the country as a public speaker. With her book's release, she could spread hope and inspiration around the world.

Lila now confidently understood that her former life did not define her. What she overcame had given her something of substance to offer others. She had processed her pain and reached a place of forgiveness. Lila now loved easily.

It helped because she knew her husband cherished her, but even more so, the relationship she had with God fueled her boldness.

Lila had many reasons to make thanksgiving a daily practice and to scream "woohoo" every chance she got. She still felt scared at times, but despite the fear, she made sure she never wasted an opportunity to express her joy. Lila felt truly blessed, and she was no longer afraid to say it.

SCREAMING WOOHOO

Men make decisions to adore and cherish their wives or abuse and manipulate them. They choose to love their spouses like Christ loves the church or to treat them like a possession they can take advantage of, in any way they want.

But women also have choices.

We can go through life with an Eeyore—"why does everything bad happen to me"—attitude, or we can squeeze every joy possible from every moment we can. Instead of feeling powerless and subsisting in victimhood, we can evaluate our options and take actions and make changes accordingly.

The kinds of actions and changes that aren't just about making us feel good but are about making the world a better place. Even hard things that happen to us can lead to a greater calling. God still transforms life's ashes into crowns of beauty for those who are willing to let Him.

For each of us, life on earth is a millionth of a second compared to eternity. Our time here is nothing in comparison to God's forever timeline.

When we get to heaven, we'll be like little kids at the birthday party who raise their hands and say, "Open mine next. Open my present, God." The gifts we offer Him will be connected to what we did for the betterment of our families, friends, communities, and fellow man or woman.

When you stand before your Maker, what will you offer the One who cherishes you beyond what you can imagine? You may not feel led to speak or write books, but what can you do to make someone else's life better?

Are you drawn to feed the helpless and hopeless? Does inspiring people to improve their health, first by setting a good example, and then sharing what you learn, something that lights you up? Are you more comfortable quietly checking on people who are going through a hard time, offering a listening ear and a shoulder to cry on? Is anonymous giving to someone in need a way you make your difference? Does picking up trash, helping clean rivers, lakes, and oceans, or other environmental endeavors turn you on? Is giving a hug to someone your way of encouraging? Do you make your difference by waving and saying hi? Or does offering a kind word to a stranger, friend, or family member light up the world?

Everything I listed is a talent, just some of the many more ways we can help the human race and our planet. While you are alive, you get one opportunity to craft your eternal gift for the One who loved you first by using the interests and talents inside you.

Let this be the moment you stop letting the past define you, defy your fear, and deliver on what you were truly made for. You ARE valuable!

We love because he first loved us.

—1 JOHN 4:19

CONCLUSION

*W*hen I decided to train for triathlons at an age most people would have said was impossible, and signed up for my first Half Ironman event, fear-based messages immediately played on my mind. Imagine, you're in minimally good shape (I did cycle) and early fifties. Who doesn't just decide to get in better shape? You think it's a great idea to take on a 1.2-mile swim that transitions to 56 miles of bike riding with about 4,000 feet of elevation and ends with a half-marathon, running 13.1 miles. That's a total of 70.3 miles. Yeah, I'm normal.

Fear told me I was nuts. Fear said, "You can't do this." Fear whispered, "You will fail."

But you know what? Fear is a liar.

During my early days of training, I was especially terrified of swimming in open water. Open-water swims still scare me, but I face that fear and control it instead of allowing it to control me.

When I started training, I knew how to keep myself from drowning, but I didn't really know how to swim. I just didn't know what I didn't know back then. I couldn't even do half a lap in a 25-yard swimming pool without complete exhaustion setting in. Tackling 84 laps felt impossible! To put that in different terms, that length is the equivalent of 1.2 miles or 2,112 yards or more than seven football fields.

Running? I'd never run more than a 5k, 3.1 miles, before training for a Half Ironman. My fear said, "You cannot accomplish this goal."

I told my fear, "Watch me."

I've learned several lessons about facing fear. Here are five points.

1. Every breathing human being has fears and anxiety, whether they admit them or not. There is nothing wrong with feeling unsure or afraid. Fear can actually warn and protect you from harm. But allowing fear to paralyze you can cause harm. The first step to freedom starts in the mind.

2. Be led by God, not driven by your fears. Look at the complete you. How can you feed your soul? Do that by healing your heart and your spirit. Pray and ask God for strength and guidance.

3. Most of what you fear will never happen. If you aren't careful, your whole life can pass you by. Many amazing opportunities can slip away with it, because you let fear drive you instead of you facing what you are afraid of and taking control of your mind.

4. Telling yourself what you *can* do instead of what you think you *can't* is a key to breakthrough. Say what you want to accomplish versus repeating what you don't

want to happen. Give attention to the positive versus the negative. What might you accomplish if you envisioned victory instead of imagining defeat?

5. Conquering fear makes you feel truly alive. Too many of us are just hanging on, barely existing, filling a void, but not making a difference. Embracing adventure, exploring the new, pursuing the quest, these are qualities our softer society is shying away from. But these very actions lead us to a fuller life. Why do I train and participate in triathlons? *Because* I'm afraid. It's crazy weird, but this is precisely what makes me feel free. Facing my fear reminds me I am breathing.

Every time I jump into an open-water swim, the distance still seems overwhelming. When you see 1.2 miles spread across a large body of water, it can overwhelm you thinking about what you need to overcome. But single-step strategies have helped me make it—one swim stroke at a time.

I look for measurement markers along the way—buoys, for instance. I tell myself to stop worrying about the full distance and focus on swimming buoy to buoy. Reaching the shorter targets fills me with a sense of accomplishment and infuses me with fresh energy that propels me toward the next goal/buoy and toward the longer distance on the horizon—the finish line.

I've completed many a swim with this methodology, but I've also used it to beat back fear and rise victorious in other areas of my life. I remind myself of something many of us have heard. How do you eat an elephant? One bite at a time.

In triathlons, safety spotters sit in kayaks to watch for swimmers who might get tangled up with leg cramps, hit a brick wall of exhaustion, or have a panic attack. I've learned that safety spotters can lessen my panicky feeling when I use them to create shorter distance goals.

These days, even though I feel afraid, I also welcome my fear. After much practice in taking control of my panicky emotions I am learning what to expect. Jumping into the water creates an instantaneous yet surreal moment where I almost feel like I'm having an out-of-body experience.

But I talk to myself. I'm scared every time, but the physical movements my body, mind, and spirit have become accustomed to help me deal with my emotions more objectively. It isn't just the fear of swimming I'm facing through my triathlon training— I'm conquering every anxiety-ridden memory embedded in my brain.

The razor-sharp words and intimidating statements leveled at me as a little girl held me back in childhood, but I push them under every time my arm enters the water. The soul-piercing wounds others have perpetrated against me are left in my wake with each pull of my arm stroke. Every person whose anger I feared or who kept me on edge wondering when they would yell at me next just drift away with each breath I exhale.

I no longer let old, current, or potential fears steal my life from me. I can now swim in open water 3,000 yards/1.7 miles without terror. When I race in a crowd, I pray for God to help me, and I self-talk my way to the finish. When another swimmer pushes into me, I tell myself that I belong here as much as anyone else, and I claim my space.

Just like I have strengthened my body, I have strengthened my fortitude.

Today, I know my mind impacts my physical actions, which in turn transforms my spirit. I have the power to control and connect my brain in healthy and healing ways.

What about you? What are your fear issues? Do they come from harassment or bullying? Are you afraid of plunging fully into a new project, idea, or process? Are the what-ifs preventing you from seeing the what-I-cans? What ghosts of your past are holding you back today?

If no one has told you this before, then let me be the first. You *can* follow your dreams. You *can* tackle what others say is impossible. You *can* control your fears and stop allowing them to control you. Set your goal, watch your target, keep reminding yourself what it will mean to achieve it, and then start moving. Your spirit will follow. Nothing feels as good as taking your life back.

I told you in the introduction that Lila reflects part of me, part of other women, and possibly, some parts of her resonate with you. She shows us truths many women struggle to believe— maybe you can relate. Do you know you are worthy of:

- processing your truest feelings,
- finding your voice,
- digging into your strength,
- taking your courage,
- accepting your value,
- overcoming through faith, and
- making a real difference in the world?

Although we live in the twenty-first century, so many women falsely think success and freedom still only happen in a man's world. But we reside in a land of opportunity.

You may have to fight for what you want, and that's appropriate as long as you do it in a healthy and respectful way, free from self-centeredness and narcissism. You have the right to seize your worth with dignity. Value yourself—dare I say—even cherish that woman you see in the mirror.

When you deny the past a place in your present, you release the potential for a happier future. No one else can decide for you. If you want change, it's up to you.

Remember, by defying fear, you silence its voice. And it no longer gets to control your life. It's OK to be vulnerable. But know that your value and worth come from God alone. Believe who He says you are.

I promise—if I can, you can too.